SUFFOLK

THE PHOTOGRAPHIC COLLECTION

Many country craftsmen combined a number of related skills. Charles Offord at Hemingstone is described on the record card accompanying this photograph as a wheelwright, but he and his predecessor Etheldred Offord were listed in directories between 1879 and 1937 as blacksmiths and proprietors of the village post office. Here he is using a drawknife. (SPS 2662)

SUFFOLK

THE PHOTOGRAPHIC COLLECTION

A COMPILATION OF
SUFFOK AT WORK & SUFFOLK

BY ROBERT MALSTER

SUTTON PUBLISHING LIMITED

This edition first published in 2003 by
Sutton Publishing Limited · Phoenix Mill
Thrupp · Stroud · Gloucestershire · GL5 2BU

Suffolk at Work was first published in 1996 by Sutton Publishing Limited
Suffolk was first published in 1997 by Sutton Publishing Limited

British Library Cataloguing in Publication Data
A catalogue record for this book is available from the British Library

ISBN 0 7509 3350 X

Typeset in 11/12pt Perpetua.
Typesetting and origination by
Sutton Publishing Limited.
Printed and bound in Great Britain by
J.H. Haynes & Co. Ltd, Sparkford.

CONTENTS

Part One – Suffolk at Work

Part Two — Suffolk

Part One
Suffolk at Work

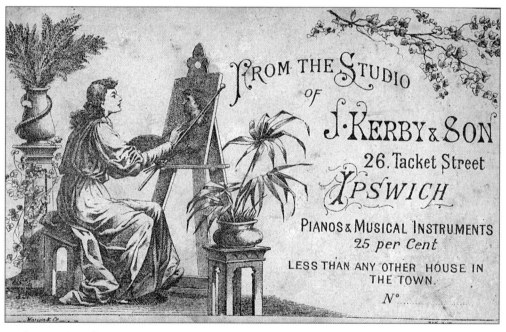

The ornate back of a carte-de-visite photograph by J. Kerby & Son, operating in the 1890s. Their studio in Tacket Street was taken over at about the turn of the century by the International Art Company and then by Louis Norman, followed by Leonard Norman.

INTRODUCTION

Suffolk has always been predominantly an agricultural county, 'one of the most skilfully tilled and most productive counties in England,' as William White described it in 1855. The majority of workers were employed on the farms, yet there were many other sources of employment.

In the Middle Ages East Anglia had been the most prosperous region of England as a result of the woollen trade. That prosperity is mirrored in the large and lavishly adorned churches, of which the best known are Lavenham and Long Melford. The economic depression which followed the collapse of the weaving trade in Suffolk can be seen reflected in the survival of so many timbered houses in Lavenham and other once-wealthy towns and villages; by the eighteenth century there was no money in these former centres of the cloth trade to build anew, and the best that could be managed was the refacing in brick of the timbered buildings.

The Census of 1831 showed that more than half the county's 61,500 families were employed in agriculture, 18,100 made a living from trade, manufacture or handicraft, and almost 12,000 were engaged in professional pursuits or were of independent means. Of the 'labouring men' 33,000 found employment in agriculture, 5,300 in handicraft and fewer than 700 in manufacturing or engineering. The change that came over the county in the course of the nineteenth century was such that at the beginning of the present century the Ipswich works of Ransomes, Sims and Jefferies alone employed some 3,000 men and boys in making steam engines, ploughs and other agricultural implements that went all over the world.

As the industries themselves expanded, the towns in which they were situated grew apace. In Ipswich and a few other centres the old was ruthlessly swept away as the new industries of engineering and artificial fertilizer manufacture brought a new prosperity during the reign of Queen Victoria. Men and women were attracted from the countryside by the prospects of employment in engineering works and factories, and not a few people came into the county from faraway places to take advantage of the new opportunities offered by industrialization; in 1841 more than 27,500 of the 315,000 inhabitants had been born outside the county.

William White quotes further from the Census of 1831 to tell us that at that time there were about 600 looms employing some 300 men in the Sudbury area making silk, velvet, satin, bunting and other similar materials, while more than 170 men and an unspecified number of women and children were employed at Haverhill, making silk fabrics for parasols and umbrellas, drabbetts for the smocks worn by many workers, and also working with Tuscan straw-plait from which ladies' bonnets were made. Straw plaiting was also carried out at Lavenham and in several other places, while textiles still had some significance along the Waveney Valley, where flax was used to produce linen cloth.

At Lavenham, Long Melford and Glemsford new trades were introduced to take the place of the long-decayed woollen cloth industry. Horsehair cloth for stiffening crinolines and for making the blinds for railway carriages was woven at Lavenham, and both there and at Long Melford, Glemsford and Hadleigh the manufacture of coconut-fibre mats became a thriving industry.

The significance of industry in what was predominantly a farming county should not be

A faded photograph of one Warne, a razor and scissor grinder who was a well-known itinerant tradesman in and around Ipswich in the latter part of the nineteenth century. Perhaps E.R. Smythe made use of this photograph, for Warne, in just this same position, features in the artist's painting of St Mary Elms. (The late Harry Wilton)

underestimated. Suffolk men from Ransomes & Rapier went out to China in 1875 to build the first railway in that country; the engines and rolling stock had been constructed in Ipswich. Milling machinery made by another Suffolk firm, Whitmore & Binyon of Wickham Market, was installed in windmills in Australia and New Zealand, and fishing vessels built in Lowestoft shipyards found their way to the Falkland Islands.

As the towns increased in size, Ipswich almost trebling its population between 1801 and 1850 and then doubling again by the end of the century, the building trades provided employment for many workers. Brickworks were to be found in almost every village, with clusters around the larger towns and a particular concentration around Sudbury, from where bricks went down the Stour by barge for shipment to London.

The railways which spread their web across Suffolk between the 1840s and the end of the century not only provided transport for bricks and the other products of the county but gave prestigious employment to many men and boys. Work on the railway was highly prized, and to be a station-master even of a country station was to hold a position of authority and of standing in the community.

Contented were those who could find steady employment on the railway, in one of the big agricultural engineering works, or in any other industry. They were assured a weekly wage, in contrast to the farmworker, the building labourer or the unskilled general labourer whose jobs were dependent on the weather as much as on seasonal demand.

Just how good 'the good old days' were for different classes of workers may be judged to some extent from the photographs in this book.

Fortunately for us, photographs showing people at work in the old trades and industries have been preserved, many of them in the Suffolk Photographic Survey, founded more than forty years ago by the Suffolk Local History Council and based firmly on the pioneering work of Bob Pratt. Other colleagues took over the task of assembling and indexing negatives and prints when Bob and Jean Pratt moved to the West Country some twenty-five years ago. The SPS, by then numbering about 8,000 photographs, was moved to the Abbot's Hall Museum of Rural Life at Stowmarket (now the Museum of East Anglian Life) where Mrs Ena Carter did sterling work researching the background to the pictures and indexing them.

Today the collection is housed in the Suffolk Record Office at Ipswich, where it provides an invaluable source of pictures for researchers from all over the country. Many of the illustrations in this book have come from the SPS, with the sanction of the Suffolk Record Office and the Suffolk Local History Council.

Others have come from the collection of the Ipswich Transport Museum, now firmly based in the Priory Heath trolleybus depot at Ipswich, from the Haverhill & District Local History Group, and from others who were generous with their help. Among them was Mr John Sayers, of the Gainsborough Silk Weaving Co. Ltd, who spent some time explaining the intricacies of his trade. With his usual generosity John Wilton provided a series of photographs on the postal services. Those not otherwise credited are from the author's collection. The selection has been somewhat arbitrary; it is impossible to cover the entire range of occupations even in two volumes (the first covers farming and fishing).

Neville Byford knotting a new warp into the loom using a knotting machine at the silk mills of the Gainsborough Silk Weaving Company at Sudbury. This complicated machine ties together the old warp threads and the new, tying some 8,000 knots in half an hour, as a preliminary to beginning a new weaving. When the firm was set up at the beginning of the twentieth century the threads had to be twisted together one by one, by hand. (Gainsborough Silk Weaving Co. Ltd)

RURAL CRAFTS

A thatched shed, said to be at Hollesley in 1889, which appears to be the workshop of a craftsman who included rakes among his products. Coppicing of woodlands produced poles that were turned by such men into handles for hoes, cromes and a variety of hand tools, were split for the making of hurdles, and were used for all kinds of purposes; the brushwood was used as fuel. (SPS 2288)

Trade card of William Ellis, who occupied premises in Bury Street, Stowmarket, for the best part of half a century. (Ivan Codd)

Robert Saunders poses in the doorway of the premises in Bury Street after having taken them over from his former employer, William Ellis, in about 1920. (Ivan Codd)

What are now regarded as typically rural crafts were once to be found in almost every town as well as in the villages of the countryside. At a time when most communities were to some extent self-supporting, a multiplicity of tradesmen played their part in supporting local life: sinking wells, making harnesses for the many working horses, doing building work, and performing any number of different tasks which have now, for better or worse, become the job of the DIY 'craftsman'.

Look in a nineteenth-century directory and you will find lists of bakers, billposters, boot and shoemakers, carpenters and joiners, dressmakers, earthenware manufacturers, fishmongers, gaiter makers, hat makers, and so on through the alphabet to whip makers, whiting manufacturers, yacht builders and zinc workers. Some of those most concerned with agriculture such as blacksmiths and wheelwrights have already been dealt with in *Suffolk at Work: Farming & Fishing*.

Every town and most villages had a saddler and harness maker who could also turn his hand to producing any other article in leather when required. When every farm had a number of horses and all road transport was horse drawn there was plenty of work for them both making new harness and repairing the old.

Arthur Pearsons, the Washbrook saddler and harness maker, at work. In the 1870s George Pearson was the village harness maker; villagers spoke of his business as 'Pearson's', and subsequent generations adopted the 's'. (SPS 2014)

Leonard Aldous, of Aldous and Hammond, the Debenham saddlers, at work on a carthorse saddle
c. 1950. (SPS 2654)

An 1879 directory lists 134 saddlers in Suffolk, and there was a saddlers' ironmonger
with premises in Ipswich and a tannery at Bures. With the decline in the use of horses
on the roads and on farms the saddlers found their trade fading away, yet fifty years later
there were still 98 at work in the county.

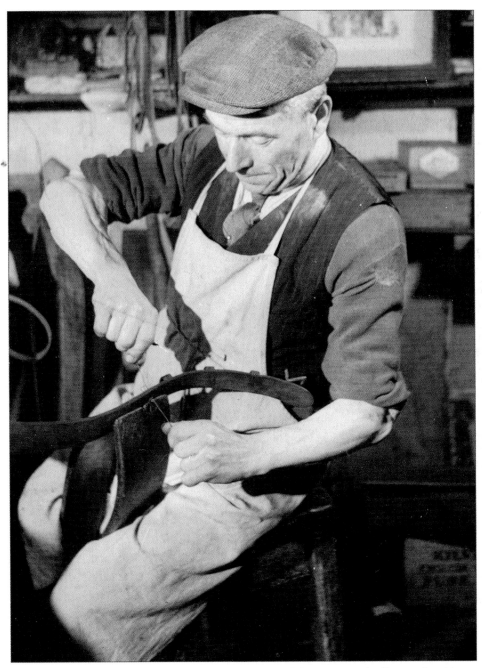

There were more than 130 saddlers and harness makers in Suffolk in 1879, and still more than 80 at work sixty years later. One of the last to continue to make a living was Mr James Garrod, whom I photographed at work in his shop in Bevan Street, Lowestoft, in the 1950s. The business had been started by his father in 1898, when local jobmasters had horses by the dozen and used them in their charabancs to take holidaymakers on trips into the country. There were many more hauling the carts which in the herring season took fish from the quays to the pickling plots and the gutting sheds. 'My father once sold a gross of whips in one day in 1913, not all to one customer but in ones and dozens,' Mr Garrod told me when I took the photograph. 'Now I don't sell one in six months.'

The premises of John George & Sons Ltd at Little Welnetham in the 1980s. The machinery appeared to have been designed by Heath Robinson, but in fact it was simple, ingenious and highly effective.

In days when hay was raked in the field by hand there was a big demand for wooden rakes, and many tradesmen used poles cut from coppice woodland to produce them. In 1892 there were six specialist producers of rakes in Suffolk, and in 1912 the firm of John George & Sons Ltd set up a rake factory beside Little Welnetham station on the Long Melford to Bury St Edmunds railway line. Describing themselves as hay rake, handle and hurdle manufacturers, the firm used ingenious machinery driven by a system of overhead shafts and belting to produce rakes, scythe stails and a variety of other articles which were sold through their London address, at 7 Laurence Poultney Hill, Cannon Street. The factory closed down about ten years ago, and the machinery has been taken to the Museum of East Anglian Life at Stowmarket, where it is currently in store.

Using a large circular saw to cut squared wood to length for the head of the rake. Some completed rakes can be seen against the wall behind the operator, who at this period seemed to be the only man working there.

Wedged into a jig, the rake head is drilled to receive the wooden tines.

A close-up view of the drilling machine, in which the rake head was advanced automatically as the drill was withdrawn after making each hole.

The head is removed from the jig after drilling.

Stephen Nunn, who describes himself on his sign as 'basket, sieve, fan and hamper maker', poses outside his Haverhill workshop with some of his products in the early years of the twentieth century. (Haverhill & District Local History Group)

Basket making was another trade which was once widespread in the county, and many were the osier beds that supplied the basket makers and sieve makers with the raw materials of their business. In some families the trade seems to have been passed on from generation to generation, and among the fifty-five basket makers in an 1879 directory there are five Parsonsons, at Bures St Mary, Clare and Sudbury, and four Markwells, at Beccles, Oakley, Saxmundham and Woodbridge. In Haverhill Stephen Nunn began his basket making business at 46 Queen Street about the turn of the twentieth century, moving to 57 High Street some twenty years later.

A rather later photograph of Stephen Nunn, on the left, with some of his workers peeling osiers at Sturmer. In the centre of the picture a youngster is pulling the wands through a metal fork to peel off the bark. (Haverhill & District Local History Group)

By the 1950s the peeling of osiers was done much more speedily by machine. In this picture Cecil Nunn and Brian Apps are preparing bunches of osiers. (Haverhill & District Local History Group)

Laying out peeled osiers to dry in a field beside the Colne Valley Railway line at Sturmer Arches, *c.* 1950. (Haverhill & District Local History Group)

OSIER &
WILLOW,
GROWERS.
BEDS,
STURMER,
ESSEX.

S. NUNN & SONS,
WHOLESALE & RETAIL
BASKET MANUFACTURERS,
57 High Street,
Haverhill, Suffolk.

A trade card of S. Nunn & Sons, showing that while their premises were in Haverhill their osier beds were on the Essex side of the Stour at Sturmer. (Haverhill & District Local History Group)

TANNING

The buildings of Combs Tannery, near Stowmarket, where the work of preparing leather was carried on for the best part of three centuries up to 1988, when the business became a victim of changing times and economic cirumstances. The photograph probably dates from about 1910.

Webb and Son, of the Combs Tannery seen in this photograph, were not only engaged in tanning but were also manufacturers of fire buckets and hoses, made (of course) of leather. (SPS 4313)

Before the days of plastics, leather was used for many purposes, and the tanning of leather was an important trade if one that was not exactly popular, because of the smells. Typical of those engaged in the trade in Suffolk was Thomas P. Hitchcock, of the Southgate Tannery, Bury St Edmunds, who advertised himself as 'wholesale manufacturer of gaiters, gloves, and leather machine bands, tanner, currier and leather dresser, wool merchant and fellmonger'. In about 1880 his firm was occupying the tannery operated forty years earlier by John Potter Everard.

A tannery which operated for the best part of 300 years until closure in 1988 was that at Combs, near Stowmarket. It was established in 1711, after Thomas Denny had advanced 'the sum of £100 to his son Thomas Denny to sink a tanyard . . .'. In 1776 the premises were let to Joseph Antrim Webb, the first of three generations with exactly the same names, and the tannery was thereafter operated by the Webb family until it was overtaken by changing times and adverse economic circumstances.

Making leather belting at the Combs Tannery, which continued to operate into the 1980s. The machinery here included an Ipswich-made beam engine, which is now at the Museum of East Anglian Life in nearby Stowmarket. (SPS 5849)

Following pages: The men of Combs Tannery, photographed on 14 November 1889. There are forty-eight men and boys in this picture; the total population of the village at the time was under 1,200. (SPS 1557)

Stacking oak bark, which was needed in large quantities for the tanning process. Much of the bark came from local woodlands.

Tannery workers seen in a photograph probably dating from the 1880s. It is not known where this and the following photographs were taken, though it is believed to be a Suffolk tannery. Below is a view of the tanpits in which the skins were immersed in water and lime, and other more noxious liquids. Tanners used to collect the contents of chamber-pots from the vicinity for use in the tanning process.

Scraping the hides to remove the hair, flesh and fat, an unpleasant job performed by skilled workers. 'The skin, when thus deprived of its moist putrescible part, and brought considerably toward the state of mere fibre, is tanned by maceration with certain astringent substances, particularly the bark of the oak tree', says an early nineteenth-century dictionary of mechanical science.

A general view of the tannery. After the skins have been cleaned, says the dictionary, they 'undergo what is properly called the tanning. This is usually done by throwing into a pit, or cistern, made in the ground, a quantity of ground oak bark that has already been used, and on this the skins and fresh bark in alternate layers, covering the whole with half a foot of tan, and treading it well down.'

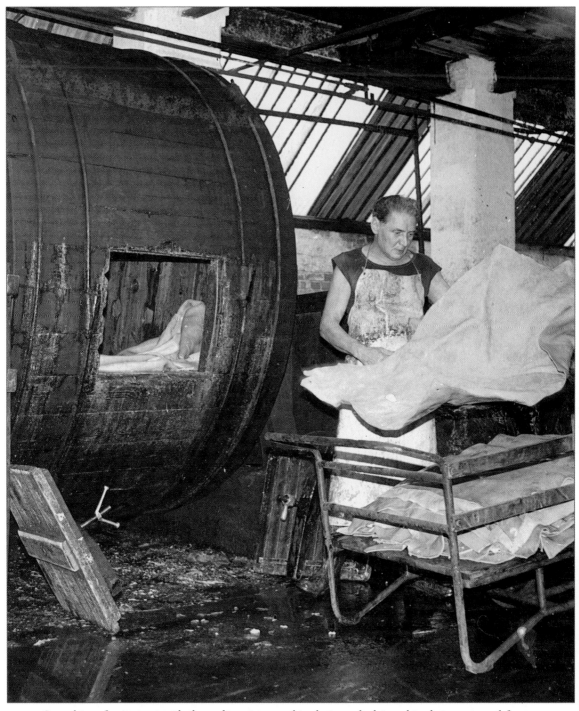

Something of a contrast with the earlier pictures, this photograph shows skins being removed from a tanning drum at the Ipswich tannery of W. & A.J. Turner, which ceased production in the 1980s. There were men still working there at the time of closure who could recall days when the contents of chamber pots were collected for use in the tanning process; such 'chemicals' were no longer used when this photograph was taken, but tanning was still a very messy and smelly operation.

CORN MILLING

The mill itself was only a major part of any complex, for apart from the miller's house there were usually cart shed, store and other ancillary buildings. Quite often one of these was an old railway carriage used as an office and sack store. This post mill at St Michael South Elmham was built in 1799 and demolished in 1955. Fred Aldridge still had the mill at work when this photograph was taken in 1939.

Barton Mills, standing beside the old Norwich–London road a mile from Mildenhall, were powered by the waters of the River Lark. In the late 1870s or 1880s, when James Howlett Godfery (so spelt) was miller, a steam engine was fitted and, probably at the same time, roller milling plant was installed. About the turn of the century the mill was taken over by Parker Brothers (Mildenhall) Ltd, who were still operating the mill by water and an oil engine some forty years later.

Millstones from the Cologne area were among the goods imported into Ipswich in the Anglo-Saxon period; mills operated either by water power or animals are mentioned in the Domesday Book. Mills were listed in connection with 178 of the 640 settlements in Suffolk. When windmills were introduced to England in the twelfth century some of the earliest were built in Suffolk; an American academic who produced a study of early windmills listed eight erected in the county by 1200.

No mills survive from these early days, though some of the watermills almost certainly occupy the same site as those listed in the Domesday survey. There was constant updating and rebuilding both of watermills and of windmills, with buildings being altered and enlarged to accommodate new machinery. In the nineteenth century the alterations to mills were sometimes made to accommodate a steam engine or later an oil engine to serve as an auxiliary to the natural power, or even to operate an additional set of machinery.

Two mills at Bungay, one a fine, powerful tower mill dated 1830 and the other a post mill of typical Suffolk pattern, with patent self-regulating sails and a fantail. The vanes in the sails were operated by the chainwheel at the rear of the mill just above the porch. These patent sails were invented in 1807 by William (later Sir William) Cubitt, who in 1812 joined Ransomes at Ipswich as their civil engineering consultant.

The miller, Ernest Gowing, and an employee pose at the roundhouse door of Sweffling mill in 1931. The mill was then operating by wind power, but a few years later it was dismantled.

Not all the flour ground in the mills was for local consumption, for there was a lively trade with London from the Suffolk ports. At Ipswich there was a whole community of mills, including a tide-mill which had a large pond filled by each succeeding high tide, grinding for 'export' to the capital; the shipping lists in nineteenth-century newspapers frequently contain references to cargoes of flour going away by sea. It was in places such as Ipswich that big mills driven by steam engines were built to take over from the smaller windmills and watermills.

A typical miller's waggon delivering to premises in Ipswich in the 1890s. William Frederick Raynham, whose name appears on the waggon, was a miller, maltster and farmer at Great Blakenham, some five miles from Ipswich. (Ipswich Transport Museum)

Haughley mill, a fine Suffolk post mill built in 1811, with members of the miller's family posing on the steps. The miller at the beginning of the twentieth century, Francis Henry Baker, also operated a steam mill. (Geoff Clarke)

The smock mill at Occold is said to have been moved at some time from Eye. The moving of mills from one site to another was by no means as uncommon as might be supposed, the old millwrights being quite capable of such operations. Usually a mill such as this would have been dismantled, but there are instances of post mills being moved complete on a timber drug or similar conveyance.

A loaded waggon stands ready to leave in this photograph of Wortham Ling mill, taken when both the post mill and the adjacent steam mill were working to capacity. The windmill was one of relatively few in Suffolk to have the fantail fitted to the buck rather than to the carriage at the base of the steps.

The post mill at Pettaugh in 1932, with the steam mill in the background. The windmill, which was rebuilt in 1865, was one of the last to work in Suffolk; it was pulled down in 1957.

Loading sacks of flour into a miller's cart at A.A. Gibbons's Westend Mills in Benezet Street, Ipswich. These big roller mills were typical of the steam-driven plants, built mainly in the towns, which were taking over from the windmills and watermills by the turn of the twentieth century. (Bob Markham)

Within a few years Gibbons's were operating both a Garrett steam waggon, registration BJ 2079 (East Suffolk), and a Thornycroft motor lorry, registration DX 1650 (Ipswich), though horses were still in evidence. The five-ton Garrett came from Leiston Works in 1914 and was named Koh-i-Noor. The Thornycroft is one of those which attracted a War Office subsidy, on condition that they were made available to the Army on the outbreak of war. (Bob Markham)

A later Garrett waggon, a four-ton undertype, went to Needham Market millers and merchants D. Quinton & Sons in 1924. Founded in the nineteenth century by Daniel Quinton, the firm is still trading in Needham Market. Here driver Bert Hearn on the left and Alf Barker pose beside the waggon, which after eleven years with Quinton's went to a new owner in Beccles. A.A. Gibbons acquired a six-ton Garrett undertype waggon in 1925.

Buxhall miller John Arthur Clover and members of his family and employees pose with the Ford Model T lorry he used to deliver flour in the Stowmarket area. The body follows the pattern of the traditional miller's waggon. Isaac Clover was a miller at Buxhall in 1844, Samuel Clover had both wind and steam flour mills there in the 1850s, and members of the Clover family continued to work the mills for almost another hundred years. (Geoff Clarke)

MALTING

A maltster using a plough to aerate the germinating barley spread on the floor of one of R. & W. Paul's big maltings at Ipswich. The 'piece' had to be regularly turned using a wooden shovel or a stick plough in order to ensure even germination and efficient aeration; in more recent times this was achieved using an electric machine not unlike a cylinder lawn-mower.

Workers at a Bury St Edmunds malting at the beginning of the twentieth century. The maltsters have either wooden malting shovels or stick ploughs, used for turning the green malt on the floor, but there are also the men responsible for stoking the furnaces under the kilns with their own implements. Malting has always been an important industry in Suffolk, closely related to the farms which produced the high-quality malting barley used.

Excellent malting barley has long been grown on Suffolk farms, so it was natural that the malting trade should have become important in the county at a very early date. In 1508 the town authorities at Ipswich restricted the trade to freemen of the borough, ordering 'that noe Forrainer alien shall by himselfe or any other, Malt any Barley, otes or other graine, under the penalty of 6s. 8d. for every quarter soe Malted'.

Malting is a process by which grain, normally barley, is changed and its constituents modified to render them soluble. The grain is first steeped in water, then allowed to germinate; during germination enzymes are developed which break down the starch in the grain into a mixture of soluble compounds. The process is completed by heating and drying the green malt in a kiln to bring the germination to an end. Whatever mechanical means may be employed to facilitate the making of malt, the process remains basically the same.

The spread of malting in the county is shown by the fact that during the 1840s there

The entrance to Snape Maltings, now famous for their link with Benjamin Britten and the Aldeburgh Festival. This arch was built in 1859 to allow a branch from the East Suffolk railway line into the complex; the date and the initials of Newson Garrett, brother of Richard Garrett of Leiston and builder of the maltings complex, can be seen on the keystone.

Malting used to be a winter occupation, since in summer the higher temperatures encouraged the growth of moulds on the malt. Many Suffolk farmworkers migrated to Burton upon Trent after harvest to work in the very large maltings there; these men photographed at Burton in 1902 are from Dennington. (SPS 1866)

were some 227 maltsters at 110 different places. With the construction of the railways and the removal in 1880 of the Malt Tax there was a great expansion of the trade, accompanied by the building of much larger malting complexes alongside railway stations and at the ports.

Until the introduction of air conditioning plant malting was a seasonal trade, carried on from October to May. This coincided with the period when little labour was required on the farm. Where malting workers did not find work on the farms they often found it in the local brickworks, for brickmaking was also a seasonal trade carried on mainly through the summer. In the twentieth century workers at the big Swonnell's maltings at Oulton Broad took work either on the buses or in holiday establishments in nearby Lowestoft.

The last floor malting in Suffolk, at Bury St Edmunds, closed in 1995, and malting is now carried on only in modern pneumatic maltings in which the barley is germinated in a deep tank, with air being pumped through the grain by fans.

The foreman maltster checks the green malt on the floor. Behind him can be seen the air-conditioning duct which controls the environment of the malting floor; before the introduction of air-conditioning the maltster could control temperature and humidity only by opening or closing the shutters on the windows – an open shutter can be seen just behind the foreman's head.

Large maltings beside the New Cut at Ipswich. Steam can be seen coming from the kilns in which the green malt was dried at the end of the germination process. This malting closed down in about 1980, and has since been converted into a business centre as part of the rejuvenation of what is now referred to as the Waterside area. The last floor malting to operate in Suffolk, at Bury St Edmunds, was demolished in 1995. Malt is now made in a relatively small number of modern pneumatic maltings.

BRICKMAKING

Brickmaking was widespread in Suffolk, making use of a variety of materials generically termed 'brickearth', and bricks, both red and white, were greatly in demand in the nineteenth century when the towns were developing apace. These brickmakers' shelters are at the brickyard at Tuddenham, near Ipswich. Each brickmaker has a pile of pallets ready to hand to receive the soft green bricks; without these the green bricks could not be handled without damage. (SPS 1563)

These brickmakers are seen in one of Charles Emeny's photographs at work in Bugg and Jolly's brickyard at Felixstowe in the 1880s. In the background black smoke pours from the top of the updraught kiln, possibly a 'Suffolk' kiln.

Probably the best record we have of any Suffolk brickworks is the series of photographs taken by a W.J. Brunell at Tuddenham St Martin in August 1900. This small country brickworks had belonged to John Luff, but by 1892 he was being described as manager of the brickworks belonging to Thomas Mortimer, an Ipswich maltster and corn and oil merchant who had other interests in the village of Tuddenham. The works closed down in 1903. The men in this photograph are mainly brickmakers, for they hold their moulds; the boys in the front row, seated on hack barrows used to take the green bricks to the hacks or drying sheds, have bricks on pallets lying on their legs. One worker has a clay spade, used to transfer pug (mixed clay) to the brickmaker's bench; its skeleton form avoids the suction which would hold clay to the blade of an ordinary spade. (SPS 2302)

Although timber frames infilled with what was known locally as wattle-and-daub was used for domestic and farm buildings until the Tudor period, the use of brick in Suffolk goes back to the twelfth century; the Norman church at Polstead has what are probably the oldest post-Roman bricks in Britain in its arcade.

More than eighty brick and tile makers are listed in an 1879 directory, but this is almost certainly an underestimate of the number of brickyards then in existence in Suffolk since estate brickworks were not listed. Woolpit is famous for the quality of its bricks, but it was by no means the only place in the county where white bricks, 'Suffolk whites', were produced.

Digging brickearth from the claypit. Both clay and sand were required for brickmaking, and fortunate indeed was the brickyard that had both materials available on site. (SPS 1559)

There were particular concentrations of brickworks in and around the larger towns, whose nineteenth-century expansion absorbed enormous quantities of bricks and tiles. Those in the Sudbury area sent large numbers of bricks down the Stour by barge for onward shipment to London, where they were used in the construction of prominent hotels and public buildings; bricks from Somerleyton were used in the building of the Royal Albert Hall and Liverpool Street station, work carried out by Lowestoft contractors Lucas Brothers, who operated the Somerleyton brickyard.

While both Somerleyton and the brickworks in the Sudbury area as well as others employed water transport, some of the larger brickworks such as those at Woolpit, Leiston and Ipswich made good use of railways, being linked to the Great Eastern Railway by branches or sidings of their own.

After about 1870 Suffolk brickmakers suffered serious competition from very large brickyards in the Peterborough area which enjoyed certain advantages, including a more central position from which to distribute large quantities of cheap bricks by rail. The blackout regulations in force during the Second World War resulted in the closure of several small brickworks in Suffolk that were using the old-fashioned updraught kilns, and only one or two remain in operation in the county.

Another view in the claypit. Clay was usually dug in the autumn so that it could be left to weather during the winter, pending a resumption of brickmaking in the spring. (SPS 2646)

A general view of the Tuddenham brickfield. Across the foreground are the hacks in which green bricks were dried out before being loaded into the kilns beyond; stocks of fired bricks await delivery in the background. (SPS 2648)

Clay and sand were mixed in this horse-operated pug mill to prepare the 'pug' which the brickmakers threw into their moulds. The material was churned by large knives inside the upright cylinder; proper mixing of the pug was necessary if the bricks were to be of uniform quality. (SPS 1560)

A brickmaker at his bench moulding bricks. In the foreground a boy wheels a barrowload of bricks away to the hacks. (SPS 1562)

Young Horace Woods stacking green bricks in the hack. Removing the pallet leaves a gap between one brick and the next, facilitating drying. If put into the kiln before drying the bricks would split as the moisture in the clay became steam. The boarded 'roof' is placed over the bricks not only to keep off rain but also to prevent the sun from drying the bricks too rapidly and causing cracking. (SPS 1564)

Workers at the brickworks that was operated by the Woolpit Brick & Tile Co. Ltd, 'manufacturers of white and red bricks, paving lumps & moulding bricks to any design & every description of Suffolk ware, a large quantity of agricultural draining pipes always in stock . . .'. The firm had offices in Moorgate Street, London. This large brickworks was in the late thirties producing bricks for the building of RAF airfields in East Anglia and for other large contracts. (Woolpit Museum P130)

Harry Woods, a brickmaker at Tuddenham, striking off the waste clay from the top of the mould, which lies on the stock affixed to the bench. The stock would often bear initials or a name to identify the yard in which the brick was made. (SPS 1561)

Dan Whitman stoking the Tuddenham kiln. A hinged door of fire-bricks is swung back from the stokehole; sometimes instead of being hinged, the door hung by a chain and could be swung aside. (SPS 1565)

Dan Whitman clearing fired bricks from the kiln; even after a week or more cooling they would still be hot to the touch. (SPS 1566)

Two workers at Woolpit standing by the stacks of 'green' bricks in the drying shed. The man on the left, a brickmaker, holds a metal brick mould, an alternative to the more usual mould made of wood. The barrow is a specially made hack barrow used to carry the bricks to the hacks and drying shed. (Woolpit Museum P281)

The horse-drawn tramway at Woolpit brickworks, which had both narrow-gauge and standard-gauge lines in operation. This narrow-gauge tramway not only linked the brickearth pits with the works but served other parts of the brickworks, and after the opening of the standard-gauge line in 1902 had a transfer siding alongside that line. (Woolpit Museum P283)

Workers with a Sentinel undertype steam lorry used by the Woolpit Brick & Tile Co. It is possible that this was one bought as surplus from one of the Ministries after the First World War, for a considerable number of steam waggons as well as motor lorries came on the market with the ending of hostilities. (Woolpit Museum P286)

The Sharp, Stewart 2–4–0 tank *Haro Haro*, built in 1870 for the Jersey Railway and bought by the Woolpit Brick & Tile Company in 1902 after serving on the construction lines in connection with the cutting of the Manchester Ship Canal. The Woolpit Company also had a small 0–6–0 saddle tank, the *Jeanie*, possibly built by Hudswell Clark. The standard-gauge line ran from the brickworks to the GER sidings at Elmswell, but seems to have ceased operation in 1916. (Woolpit Museum P287)

Following pages: Workmen in a gravel pit in the 1920s, with a horse-operated tramway of the kind used in many brickyards to bring clay to the pug mill. It has been suggested that this is Fison & Company's Finborough Road brickworks at Stowmarket, but the identification is uncertain. (Mrs Margaret Gooderham)

The brickworks at Holbrook Creek, on the north bank of the Stour estuary. This works, with its big continuous-burning kiln, was established at about the turn of the century and went out of production in the early twenties. When the Royal Hospital School was being built nearby between 1929 and 1933, building materials had to be landed by barge at the creek (see page 77).

BUILDING TRADES

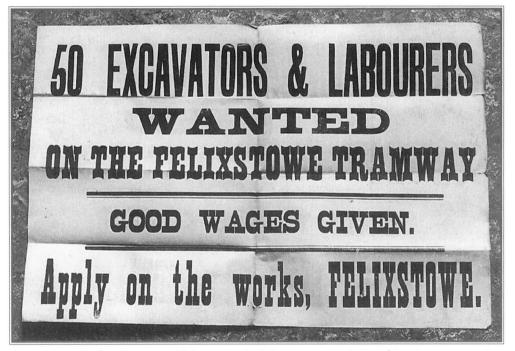

A bill advertising for excavators and labourers on the 'Felixstowe Tramway', one of the schemes promoted in the 1870s by George Tomline of Orwell Park, Nacton. Local printers were always able to supply such bills, printed with wooden type on machines that would now be considered most old-fashioned.

Conditions on the site of Felixstowe Dock, brainchild of an enigmatic Victorian landowner often known as Colonel Tomline, were none too pleasant for those employed on the scheme. Perhaps it is not surprising that when excavation of the dock basin began in November 1881 progress was painfully slow; it came to a halt in 1882 when the contractor became insolvent, and the dock was not opened until 1886. (Suffolk Record Office)

Construction workers had a vital part to play in the expansion of industry and the infrastructure that underpinned Victorian trade and commerce. There are no photographs to show the men who built the first railways in Suffolk in the 1840s, but later civil engineering ventures such as the construction of Felixstowe Dock in the 1880s are recorded.

Changes there have been, particularly in the field of safety at work, though employment in the construction industry still demands stamina as well as skill. In the nineteenth century the cost of large projects was counted in lives as well as in cash, for working practices were often incredibly haphazard and downright hazardous.

Mechanical excavating equipment is nowhere to be seen in this photograph of the Felixstowe excavation, though a narrow-gauge tramway has been laid to cart away the spoil shovelled up by hand. (Suffolk Record Office)

Building workers line the wooden scaffolding during work on Felixstowe Lodge, a large house at Felixstowe designed by Robert Schultz for Felix Thornley Cobbold in 1902. (SPS 257)

A steam crane and the boiler of a steam pump are to be seen in this postcard of work on the rebuilding of Southwold Harbour, *c.* 1907. The town council hoped that by improving the facilities it would attract drifters taking part in the East Anglian herring fishery, but the outbreak of war in 1914 put paid to such ambitions. (Suffolk Record Office)

The building of new premises at Holbrook for the Royal Hospital School in the early 1930s was a very big contract for Garrard & Sons Ltd. This view, taken on 21 April 1932, shows work on the main building. On the opposite page is an advertisement of 1875 for the Ipswich firm of E. & E.C. Gibbons, who were not only builders and contractors but also brickmakers at Ipswich and Shotley.

In place of the timber scaffolding seen in earlier photographs, the scaffolding used in the construction of a water tower at Rushmere St Andrew, near Ipswich, in 1972 is of metal. The erection of such scaffolding was a task requiring considerable skill.

The bricklayer's skills were not confined to the use of the trowel. Stowmarket photographer George Wilden took this shot of a bricklayer catching bricks lobbed to him by a fellow-worker below. (Geoff Clarke)

In contrast to the lack of equipment evident in earlier photographs, any modern building site is overshadowed by a tower crane for handling materials. This is the Buttermarket site at Ipswich in the early 1990s.

ROPEMAKING

Gowing's rope-walk at Lowestoft seen in an engraving of 1872. A 'patent ropery' had been established by the Gowing family in 1790, and the concern remained in the family for more than 100 years before being overtaken by the bigger producers in towns such as Bridport.

Workers at the Haverhill Rope, Twine and Sack Company in the 1920s. At the left are William Whiting, with sack apron, and Bertram Radford, who were partners in the firm, and on the right of the line is Walter Mayes. Behind them is the rope-walk, which seems to have dated from about 1893 when James Henderson was running a 'rope works'. (Haverhill & District Local History Group)

In the days of sail enormous quantities of rope were needed for the rigging of ships, and there were many rope walks at the ports. In about 1880 there were at least ten ropemakers in Lowestoft, two each in Southwold and Woodbridge, one at Aldeburgh and others in Ipswich, but rope-walks were not found only on the coast.

Carters, farmers and others also needed both ropes and twine, and rope and twine makers were found at places such as Stowmarket, Bury St Edmunds, Long Melford and Sudbury. Plough lines, halter shanks, cart ropes, cowbands and other things were made for agricultural use, besides scaffold ropes, bell ropes and all kinds of other ropes for special uses.

Ropemakers were also able to turn their hands to such tasks as the making of waterproof canvas covers for protecting farm machinery and the like, net making and the weaving of halter heads, bellybands and straps. In some cases the manufacture of sacks was undertaken, as it was by the appropriately named Haverhill Rope, Twine and Sack Company.

Looking along the rope-walk, a long and rather crude wooden building with a roof of corrugated iron. (Haverhill & District Local History Group)

A range of ex-army huts laid end to end later provided a new rope-walk at Haverhill. William Whiting and Bertram Radford are again seen on the left with, left to right, William Mayes, Bertram Whiting, an unnamed youngster, Percy Whiting, George Sizer, James Downey, another whose name is unknown, and Walter Mayes. The machinery from this rope-walk can now be seen in the Boby Building at the Museum of East Anglian Life, Stowmarket. (Haverhill & District Local History Group)

TEXTILES & CLOTHING

Workers at the Ipswich flax factory, photographed by Robert Burrows in 1858. (Suffolk Record Office)

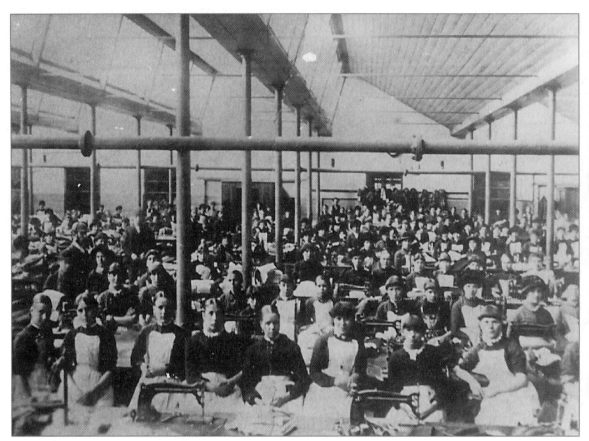

Workers in the sewing room at Gurteen's Chauntry Mills, Haverhill, before the turn of the twentieth century. Their sewing machines were treadle-operated, but in other parts of the mills were power looms worked by a steam engine named Caroline after a member of the Gurteen family. (Haverhill & District Local History Group)

During the Middle Ages Suffolk became one of the most prosperous counties in the country as a result of the woollen trade. The decline of this trade was evident as early as the seventeenth century, but in the eighteenth its place was filled to some extent by the arrival of the silk industry, which moved from Spitalfields into the rural areas, particularly to the Sudbury area. Horsehair weaving and the making of coir mats took over at places like Hadleigh and Lavenham.

The manufacture of clothing was at one time widespread in the county, one Bury St Edmunds firm having 'manufactories' in the depth of the countryside at Barrow, Chevington and Cowlinge. The most important firm of all was Gurteen & Sons, whose business had been built up on the production of smocks and other working clothing and who in 1879 employed upwards of 2,500 people at Haverhill; at that time the population of the town was little more than 3,000.

A view across the rooftops of Chauntry Mills taken in about 1889 from the tower of Haverhill parish church. In the distance can be seen one of the town's windmills. (Haverhill & District Local History Group)

Two photographs of Chauntry Mills taken in the 1930s. Above are some of the Henderson hair looms, with Mrs Ted Basham in the right foreground, and below is part of the main sewing machine room. (Haverhill & District Local History Group)

Caroline, the Chauntry Mills steam engine, at work. In a nineteenth-century directory Gurteen & Sons were described as 'manufacturers by steam power of drabbets & various cotton & linen fabrics; also wholesale & export clothiers'.

Two pictures of Reginald Warner, founder of the Gainsborough Silk Weaving Company, in the company's premises in Priory Walk, Sudbury, *c*. 1906. Having been apprenticed to the English Silk Weaving Company at Ipswich when he was thirteen, he set up his own firm at Sudbury at the age of twenty-three with hand looms acquired from weavers' houses in the town. On the opposite page he stands proudly among the looms, and in the picture above he is climbing the stairs to his office, seen in the background. It is said that he took these photographs himself, using some form of remote control. (Gainsborough Silk Weaving Co. Ltd)

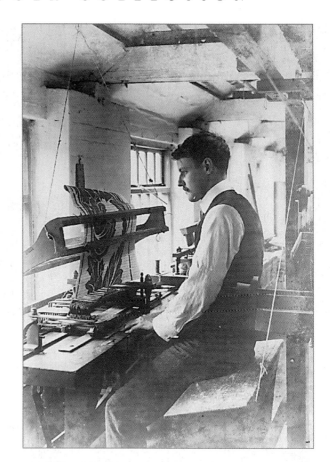

Reginald Warner sitting at a treadle-operated card punching machine. Holes punched in the painted draft controlled the Jacquard loom, automatically producing the intricate weaving pattern. (Gainsborough Silk Weaving Co. Ltd)

Winding warp yarn from skein to bobbin in the new premises on the outskirts of Sudbury to which the firm moved in 1925. (Gainsborough Silk Weaving Co. Ltd)

Freddie Mills weaving a silk damask on a pressure harness loom, which works on the same principle as the hand looms used in the early days of the company. Freddie, who worked for the firm for around half a century, was well known in the area as a cricketer, playing both for Sudbury Town and for the works team. (Gainsborough Silk Weaving Co. Ltd)

Mrs E. Cook carries out a visual inspection of a length of material to ensure that it is perfect. In her right hand is a small pair of shears. Inspection of the finished article is vital in the production of very high quality materials. (Gainsborough Silk Weaving Co. Ltd)

ENGINEERING

Not so much people at work as people at play: the only known picture of the old foundry of Ransome & Son in Ipswich. The firm gave up the old foundry in 1849 when it completed the move to a new works beside the Wet Dock. (Ransomes, Sims & Jefferies)

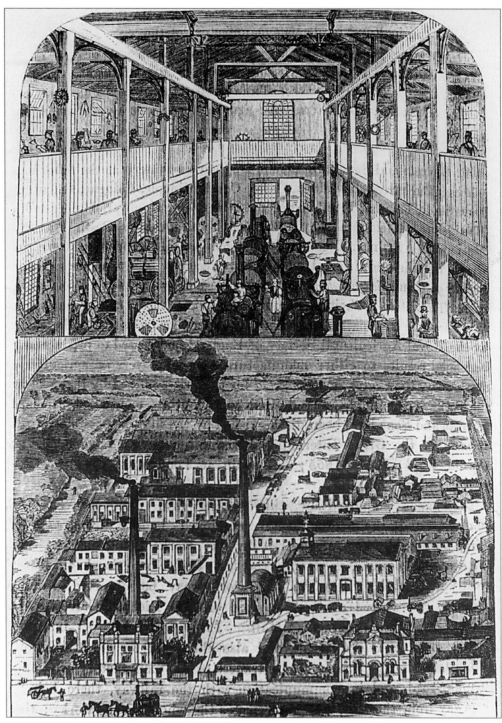

An artist's impression of Leiston Works from the *Great Eastern Railway Guide*, 1860. Although one has to make allowance for artistic licence, the lower picture gives a fair impression of the extent of the Garrett works at that time. The upper picture shows the interior of the Long Shop, built in 1852–3 as an erection shop for steam engines, then forming an increasingly important part of the firm's output.

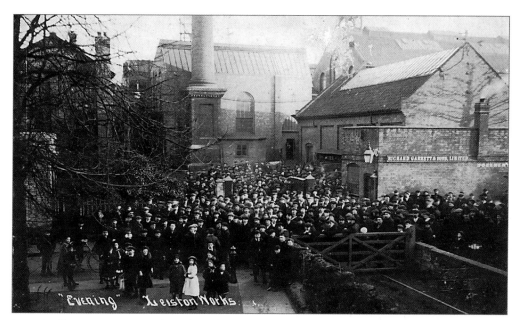

Leaving-off time at Leiston Works in the early years of the twentieth century. In the ordinary way progress homewards was much more rapid, but the workmen – and the children – have paused to pose for the local photographer, J.S. Waddell. In the right background is the Long Shop, now the centrepiece of the Long Shop Museum.

Richard Garrett, the third of that name to be head of the Leiston company, was much involved with the setting up of the Great Exhibition in 1851. When the exhibition was open in Hyde Park, employees from Leiston Works were taken to London in two of the ships belonging to the Garretts which were moored at Horseferry Wharf, where they served as floating hostels for the period of the visit. Here the workers and their families are seen setting off from Horseferry Wharf for Hyde Park behind a brass band.

It was the manufacture of agricultural implements that provided the basis for the growth of engineering in Suffolk. 'There is no part of England where the implements of agriculture are more perfect than in Suffolk, or where new implements are tried with more readiness and less prejudice', as a nineteenth-century writer put it. 'This is owing in a very great measure to the very excellent manufacturers of agricultural implements who live in the county.'

In 1778 Richard Garrett, the son of a Woodbridge bladesmith, set up in business in Leiston as a sickle and edge tool maker and bladesmith, thus laying the foundations of a firm that was to achieve fame as a producer of thrashing machines and other agricultural machinery. And eleven years later Robert Ransome moved from Norwich to Ipswich and set up an iron foundry in St Margaret's Ditches, where he carried on the production of ploughshares and other necessities for the farmer.

The improvements that Robert Ransome made in the design and casting of ploughshares and the developments in plough technology inaugurated by his three sons and their successors were to be as much part of the history of agriculture as they were part of the Suffolk story. With the agricultural depression that followed the ending of the wars with France, Ransomes branched out into civil engineering; then with the coming of the railways they diversified into the manufacture of railway materials.

Only when the growth of their export trade in agricultural implements necessitated an expansion of the works did they hive off the railway department to a new company, Ransomes & Rapier, with a separate works on the other side of the Orwell. R & R, as they were known in Ipswich, were to build the first railway in China as well as other narrow-gauge railways in other parts of the world.

These were high-profile companies whose names became known the world over, but there were other smaller firms who were little less prominent in their fields. At Stowmarket Woods & Co, founded in about 1812 by James Woods, could by the end of the century claim to be 'engineers, manufacturers of general agricultural, hydraulic & steam machinery, millwrights, wagon and cart builders, target makers, &c. &c.'.

At Wickham Market Whitmore & Binyon had 'a great reputation for the production of steam engines, water wheels, windmills, and machinery, and more especially such as are adapted for corn and flour mills'. When roller mills began to replace the old-fashioned stone mills Whitmore's, along with the Ipswich firm of E.R. & F. Turner, quickly achieved a premier position in the new technology, building equipment that went into new mills all over the country.

Special machinery for the dressing of seed was the speciality of Robert Boby at Bury St Edmunds, who from being general agricultural engineers became closely concerned with the malting and brewing trades. The bobycart, a special kind of trolley with two five-foot wooden wheels used to spread barley on the malting floor after it had been steeped, took its name from the firm that made it.

The boiler shop at the Richard Garrett works at Leiston, *c.* 1913. The one-eyed man in the foreground is William Booty, who had been an apprentice from 1852 to 1859 and was employed in the works on and off for much of his life. He lost an eye in an accident in 1904 but remained at work in the boiler shop until his death in 1914. Below is the ground floor of the Long Shop at Leiston Works in the first decade of the twentieth century, with the machines driven by belting from the overhead shafts. The Long Shop is believed to be one of the earliest flow-line assembly halls in the world; it is a grade II listed building. The short man third from left is said to be William Frost, who because of his small stature was nicknamed 'Giant'. (Both R.A. Whitehead)

When Ransomes moved from the Old Foundry to a new dockside works in 1849 the move was celebrated with a great dinner in one of the newly erected shops for the workmen and invited guests. The motto for this event, at which prodigious amounts of food and drink were consumed, was 'Success to the Plough and Rail', an appropriate amendment of the popular public house sign The Plough and Sail since the firm was then greatly concerned with both agricultural implements and railway materials. The story of how the new works came into being is a rather amusing one, as recalled by William Worby, later the works manager: 'One morning in March, 1837, I was summoned to the presence of Messrs. Robert and James Ransome in Mr. Robert Ransome's room, which was then an upper room in the offices in St. Margaret's Ditches. Mr. Robert Ransome told me that they had sent for me to tell me to find a place for myself.' Poor Worby thought he was being given the sack. 'I asked them if they wanted me to leave them, whereupon Mr. Robert Ransome said, "By no means – we mean that you should go and hire malt offices or some such place, where you can take some of the men and some of the work, forming a sort of branch works, as we are getting too thick here . . .".'. (Ransomes, Sims & Jefferies)

Previous page: Millwrights Whitmore & Binyon not only constructed mills in Britain but had an extensive overseas business. Their works at Wickham Market, seen here in an artist's impression of about 1875, included its own gasworks. The firm was founded by John Whitmore in 1780, and came to a sudden end in 1901; the works and equipment were sold over four days, the catalogue of the sale including 'The Loose Tools for Turners, Fitters, Boilermakers, Ironfounders and Smiths for between 200 and 300 hands', an indication of the size of the workforce.

"STEEL CHILL" DIGGING PLOUGHS.

T.C.P. & T.C.P.H.

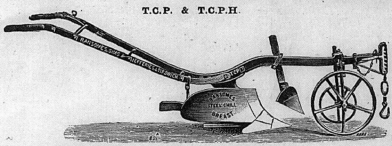

These Ploughs will plough a greater depth and width than any ordinary Plough with less draught, and will turn a furrow up to 10 in. or 12 in. wide, breaking the furrow slice to the bottom.

The breasts or mould boards are made of chilled cast iron which is harder than steel, and the surface is so thoroughly glazed that no soil will adhere to it. The share is made in three parts, the wing and point, being separate, are renewable at a small cost, and the chilled cutter, instead of the ordinary coulter, is also renewable These Ploughs will answer admirably for :—

Ploughing stubble or lea land. Paring or Skimming and burying twitch and weeds.

Cross ploughing and ploughing for all kinds of green crops. "Moulding" up Hops in the Autumn, and "Ploughing back" in the Spring. Deep ploughing in market gardens.

Ploughing in fruit grounds between rows of raspberry canes, currant and gooseberry bushes, &c., &c.

The standard fitting is with two wheels, steel chill breast, single knife tail piece and skim coulter.

Mark.		Weight.	Mark.		Weight.
T.C.P.	...	**241 lbs.**	**T.C.P.H.**	...	**262 lbs.**

The following extras can be supplied :—Double Knife Tail Piece, Ridging Body, Potato Body with Front Raisers and Hind Prongs, also Body for ordinary work with Cast or Steel Breast as desired.

"STEEL CHILL" DIGGING PLOUGH.

I R.C.P.

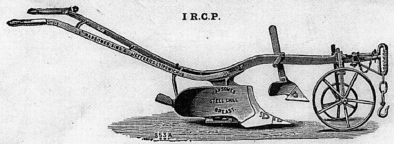

This Plough will turn either deep or shallow furrows, leaving the soil thoroughly pulverised and all the weeds entirely buried ; so that the land is ready for immediate sowing, even harrowing being often unnecessary. It will work equally well on either heavy clay, loamy or light soils, or on stubble or clover ley.

It is light in draught and turns a furrow up to 12 in. wide and all wearing parts are of chilled cast-iron (harder than steel) and the more they are used the brighter and cleaner they scour.

The standard fitting is with two wheels, steel chilled breast, skim coulter and single knife tail piece.

Mark.					Weight.
I.R.C.P.	...	...	...	...	**245 lbs.**

The following extras can be supplied :—Ridging Body, Potato Body, with Front Raisers and Hind Prongs, also Body for ordinary work with Cast or Steel Breast as desired.

Robert Ransome built up his business on the excellence of his ploughs, taking out a number of patents including one for chilled iron ploughshares. The firm continued to build ploughs, among many other things, until quite recent years but is now concerned only with grass machinery. This is a page from a 1921 catalogue. (Ransomes, Sims & Jefferies)

Ransomes, Sims & Jefferies built up a very large export trade in steam engines and agricultural implements, and it was to make space for the expansion of this side of the business that the railway materials department was hived off in 1869 to a new company, Ransomes & Rapier. To promote their overseas trade RS & J took space at many trade fairs and agricultural shows, like this one at Melbourne in 1901. (Ransomes, Sims & Jefferies)

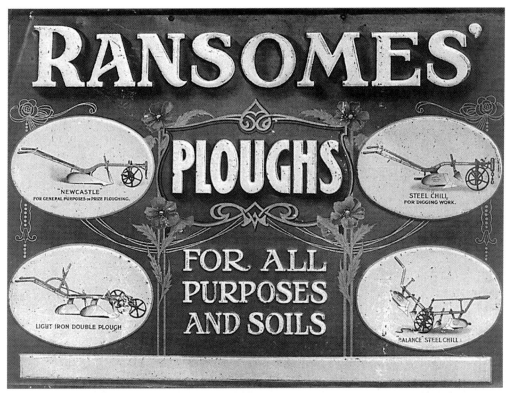

A sheet-metal advertisement for Ransomes' ploughs.

Men of Ransomes' Plough Works don their Sunday best for an outing in 1910. The group photograph was taken by Harry Walters, a photographer who had his studio on St Margaret's Plain, Ipswich.

During the First World War Ransomes and Garretts were among the firms entrusted with the building of aircraft for the Royal Flying Corps. Here are Ransomes employees posing with an FE2B fighter in one of the hastily erected hangars in Fore Hamlet, Ipswich, in which the aircraft were built.

In this century RS & J took an interest in electric vehicles, and in 1924 built its first trolleybus for Ipswich Corporation Transport. The firm supplied fifteen more to the Corporation in 1926, then in 1933 built a number of double-deckers for Ipswich, besides others for undertakings in other parts of the country. Trolleybuses were also built for service in a number of other countries.

Sir Richard Rapier, a partner in Ransomes & Rapier, of Waterside Works, Ipswich, harboured an ambition to construct the first railway in China. He achieved his ambition in 1875–6, when a number of Ipswich men went out to China to build the Shanghai and Woosung Railway, which was operated successfully for three years until the mandarins purchased the line and closed it down. The two Ipswich-built engines, the Flowery Land on the left and the Celestial Empire on the turntable, are seen here at the depot at Shanghai.

The lower picture on the opposite page shows one of the first mobile cranes made by Ransomes & Rapier in use at Waterside Works to load the firm's Chevrolet lorry, c. 1924. A spring balance is interposed between the crane hook and the sling carrying the load. (Ipswich Transport Museum)

In later years Ransomes & Rapier turned to the production of sluice gear which went all over the world. Here a set of sluices for a barrage on the Nile is ready to leave Waterside Works in the 1920s.

At the Suffolk Iron Works at Stowmarket Woods, Cocksedge & Co. produced a variety of agricultural implements and, between 1862 and 1896, steam engines of various kinds. The Suffolk Iron Works was laid out on what had once been garden ground behind the houses and shops in Bury Street, Stowmarket. The entrance to the works, which included a foundry, woodworking shops, fitting shops and other buildings for storage of both raw materials and products, can be seen on the left of this photograph, which appears to date from the 1890s; by then J.S. Cocksedge had left the firm to set up his own business in Ipswich. The advertisement on the opposite page shows a portable engine of a kind widely used on farms both in this country and in the colonies; it could be moved from place to place by horses. (Ivan Codd)

On following pages: The interior of an iron foundry, that of Richard Garrett Engineering Ltd at Leiston, seen at about the time the company celebrated its bicentenary in 1978. Unhappily the company closed down not very long afterwards.

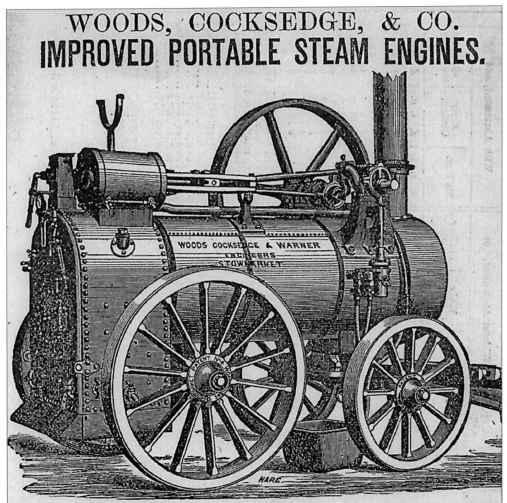
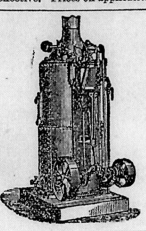

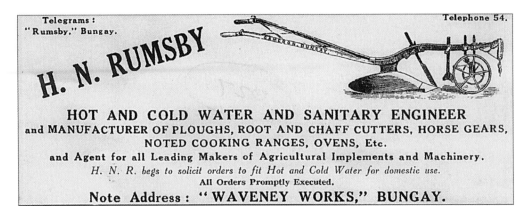

A 1929 advertisement for Harry N. Rumsby, of Earsham Street, Bungay, one of the lesser engineering firms that existed in Suffolk's small towns. Established by Daniel Cameron at least by 1820, the firm produced a plough that gained sufficient reputation to be exported to the colonies. Below is an advertisement for Robert Boby, a firm that became so well known for seed screening machines that it is said that the expression 'to boby the seed' entered the local dialect in Lincolnshire.

Robert Boby set up in business as an ironmonger in the 1850s, and within a few years had become a manufacturer of agricultural implements with a works on the St Andrew's Street South site that the firm was to occupy for many years. By the 1920s the firm was described as 'patentees of the Boby corn screens & manufacturers of grain, malt & seed cleaning & refrigerating machines, elevators, conveyors, castings &c.; malting & brewery engineers' at St Andrew's Works. Their telegraphic address proclaimed their fame as makers of seed cleaners; it was simply 'Screens'.

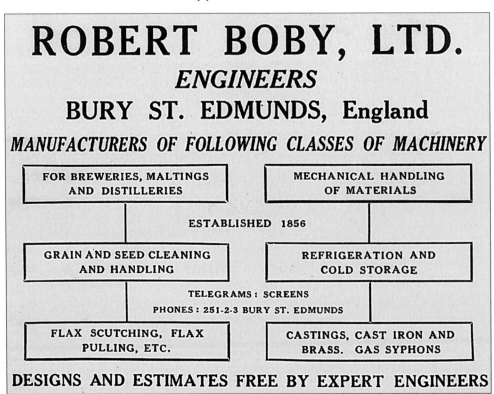

TRANSPORT

A job on the railway was considered a plum job; uniform was provided and if all went well it was employment for life. These three Great Eastern Railway station staff seem to feel that they have much to be thankful for.
(Ipswich Transport Museum)

A road-making gang at work on a road running under the Ipswich–Bury St Edmunds railway line near Tostock in the early years of the century. The nearest engine is thought to be a Tasker 'Little Giant' steam tractor, possibly belonging to Downing Brothers, engineers and machine owners of nearby Norton. Tarmacadam had not yet come into use, and the Aveling and Porter steamroller was used to bind the loose stones into a reasonably solid road surface; the water cart beyond sprinkled the roadway to help the material bind together. (Woolpit Bygones Museum)

Before 1914 the horse was the essential prime mover. The railways had steam engines, of course, but when it came to delivering parcels the railway companies used horse vans, and the railway stables were in many cases among the larger such complexes in a town. For men employed with horses the day began early, as the horses had to be fed and groomed before work started.

In an age when regular employment was the key to a reasonable way of life a job on the railway tended to be regarded as a privileged occupation. A man might start as a porter or signalman and work his way up to station-master; others started as engine cleaners, then trained as firemen and eventually found rewarding and satisfying, if far from comfortable, work as drivers.

A horse-drawn pantechnicon belonging to Frasers Ipswich Ltd, still in use in the 1920s. The advertisement of R.D. & J.B. Fraser, who claimed to have been established as long ago as 1833, in an Ipswich directory showed a similar vehicle bearing the slogan 'By Road or Rail' mounted on a flat railway truck. Fraser's store in Princes Street, Ipswich, was a well-known landmark on the way from the station into the town. Below is an advertisement from the Suffolk County Handbook of 1904 for a Felixstowe jobmaster and carter, showing a pantechnicon with large rear wheels and a well to accommodate tall items of furniture. (Ipswich Transport Museum)

An early Thornycroft motor lorry operated by the Great Eastern Railway Company, with its crew. Their boots, as well as the solid tyres of the lorry, provide evidence of the muddy state of the road. (Bob Markham)

The staff of Orwell station on the Felixstowe branch, built by Lucas Brothers for George Tomline in 1876 and taken over by the Great Eastern some years later, with the station-master on the right. Orwell was the station for Orwell Park, and was obviously sited for Tomline's own convenience; legend has it that in the early days the staff wore Tomline's livery, but this does not necessarily mean that they were dressed as footmen in silk breeches and stockings. (Ipswich Transport Museum)

Driver and fireman of Great Eastern Y14 no. 566 (later LNER J15 no. 65464) pose on the engine at Long Melford. The headcode, a red disc on top of the firebox and a green one on the right-hand side of the buffer beam, indicates that the train was working along the Marks Tey, Sudbury and Bury St Edmunds line. At Long Melford Junction it would leave the Stour Valley line to head north through Lavenham to Bury. A great deal of excellent work was done on East Anglian lines by 0–6–0 engines of this kind. (Ipswich Transport Museum)

THE ROYAL MAIL

Many village stores were also post offices, like this one at Norton kept by Edward Mickleburgh Easter from the beginning of the twentieth century until the mid-twenties. The car in this photograph, dated 1907, is a De Dion Bouton. (John Wilton)

George Brame became one of the first letter carriers in Ipswich in 1839, when William Stevenson Fitch was the Ipswich postmaster. The post office was in a small room at the back of Fitch's chemist shop, on the corner of Buttermarket and The Thoroughfare. (John Wilton)

The postal staff at Woolpit post office setting out on their rounds, two on bicycles and two on foot. (John Wilton)

The General Post Office came into existence under an Act of Parliament passed in 1656, though the Royal Mail's monopoly of the inland post goes back even further, to 1609. It was not until 1840 that Roland Hill was responsible for the introduction of the Penny Post, using self-adhesive stamps as proof of payment of the standard fee. The massive movements of population in Victoria's reign and the rise in the level of literacy together boosted the popularity of the postal service, which became a highly efficient means of communication for all classes of people.

The Post Office provided steady employment for those who were prepared to work what we today would call unsocial hours. The work of a postman was very hard, and not particularly well paid, but many men started their careers as messengers at the age of fourteen or so, became postmen, and went on to spend their whole working lives in the service. It was a 'respectable' job in an age when respectability was most important; the uniform gave the wearer prestige among his neighbours, and even if the wages of no more than thirty shillings a week at the end of the nineteenth century were less than those of a skilled craftsman, there were plenty of men prepared to put up with the strict discipline of the GPO and the long hours for the sake of secure employment.

The postmen at Needham Market at about the turn of the twentieth century, with head postman Mr Prime seated in the middle. (John Wilton)

Robert Burwood, a postman at Orford at the beginning of the twentieth century. (John Wilton)

The staff gather outside the post office at Wangford, near Southwold, as the mail cart prepares to take the outgoing mail to Halesworth. The bare-headed man in the doorway is probably Robert Homersham, the sub-postmaster. (John Wilton)

In 1907 the motor coach that had superseded the four-horse London–Colchester coaches was extended to Ipswich to carry road-borne parcels: these bore the rubber stamp 'Coach road-borne'. (John Wilton)

A baker's dozen of postmen about to begin the morning delivery at Bury St Edmunds; the time is approaching a quarter past seven. (John Wilton)

Besides delivering the Royal Mail the Post Office was responsible for the telegraph service by which urgent messages could be sent from town to town, before the days of a national telephone system. Many boys began a lifetime with the Post Office as telegraph messengers; these youngsters were photographed at the back of the post office on the Cornhill at Bury St Edmunds in about 1898 with the postmaster, Mr Knights, the chief of the instruments room, Mr W.G. Powell, and the post office cat. (John Wilton)

D. Gray became a messenger at Ipswich at about the time of the First World War. He retired from the Post Office in 1966. (John Wilton)

Part Two
Suffolk

A timeless scene: the watersplash at Kersey.

'In the Barley-Harvest', one of the Suffolk photographs by Peter Henry Emerson published in his *Pictures of East Anglian Life* in 1888. Emerson, sometimes described as 'the father of naturalistic photography', produced some of the finest Victorian photographs of work on the land.

INTRODUCTION

Until local government was reorganized in 1974 Suffolk had always been a divided county. The separation of west and east went far back into history, to the time when Edward the Confessor gave to Bury St Edmunds Abbey jurisdiction over the eight and a half hundreds known as the Liberty of St Edmund. This was to become West Suffolk. Another abbey, that of Ely, had jurisdiction in five and a half hundreds known as the Liberty of St Etheldreda or the Wicklaw, in the south-east of the county around Woodbridge. In spite of the changes brought about by the dissolution of the monasteries, the Wicklaw continued to be something of a law unto itself until it became part of East Suffolk on the setting up of county councils.

Even after more than twenty years as a unified county, Suffolk still has something of a dual personality; there are still features which enable one to discover the old boundary between east and west. Though Ipswich is now the county town, Bury St Edmunds has administrative offices belonging to the county council and a character that refuses to admit its reduced status.

Although predominantly an agricultural county, Suffolk has throughout its history had its share of industry. In the Middle Ages it was one of the most prosperous areas of the kingdom, for its merchants grew rich on the sale of its woollens, and tourists come today to seek out reminders of the trade that enabled men to seek personal salvation through the building of great churches like those of Long Melford and Lavenham. The weaving trade fell on hard times, but other industries such as malting, engineering and the making of agricultural implements, and the manufacture of clothing have played their part in ensuring that Suffolk has not been solely dependent on farming for employment and wealth.

Suffolk was fortunate in having a surprising number of early photographers, both amateurs and professionals, who delighted in recording the county in which they lived. Their work has left us with a rich heritage of pictures showing much that has disappeared in the past hundred years, and a great deal that has changed.

One of the very earliest amateur photographers to work in the county was Richard Dykes Alexander (1788–1865), a partner in the Ipswich bank of Alexander & Company. A member of a Quaker family, he was related to members of the Dillwyn and Sims families who were involved with the Ransomes in the manufacture of agricultural implements and other things at Ipswich, so it is not surprising that some of his photographs are of steam engines produced by their firm.

To produce a negative he used fine-textured paper which was waxed and then soaked in a solution of potassium iodide. When the paper was to be sensitized it had to be passed through a solution of silver nitrate, washed in distilled water and dried between sheets of blotting paper.

Long exposures were needed with this process, sometimes a quarter of an hour or even more. The disadvantage was that people passing by did not appear on the completed picture, but an advantage was that the photographer could appear in his own photograph by removing the lens cap, walking round and sitting down in the field of view, keeping very still for the length of the exposure and then getting up to replace the lens cap at the end of the time. It is possible that some pictures showing Richard Dykes Alexander himself were taken in this way.

Many photographs taken in the 1850s and 1860s by Alexander surfaced in 1978 when they were sent

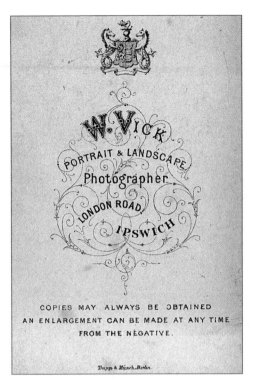

The back of a *carte-de-visite* portrait photograph by William Vick (1833–1911), who took over the Ipswich business of William Cobb *c*. 1870.

to Sotheby's Belgravia for inclusion in a sale of photographic images and related material. Fortunately it was possible for Suffolk Record Office to acquire some of these early pictures, and I have been privileged to include a number of these.

An Ipswich professional artist, Robert Burrows (1810–83), was another who espoused photography in the 1850s, possibly seeing it as an aid to his painting but more likely, on the evidence of what remains, enjoying the new medium for its own sake. An album of small prints made by him is also in the Suffolk Record Office.

Several of the photographs in the early part of this book were taken by an influential amateur, George Christopher Davies (1849–1922), a young Shropshire-born solicitor who was attracted to East Anglia by the lure of the Broads, of which he had read in an article in *The Field*. 'Part of the equipment of a yacht is a photographic camera,' he wrote in 1883, and he and some cruising friends seem to have made good use of theirs while sailing the Broadland waterways. Davies himself published a series of photogravures in the 1880s as well as illustrating his own books.

By 1879 there were no fewer than thirty-one professional photographers, one woman among them, listed in Kelly & Company's *Post Office Directory of Suffolk*, but photography had by then passed its infancy. The home-made paper negative and the daguerreotype had largely given way to the glass plate negative and the bromide printing paper.

Among those professionals was William Vick (1833–1911). He arrived in Ipswich in about 1870 to take over the business of William Cobb, who had described himself in the previous decade as a photographic artist. Vick took many portraits in his studio at Barrack Corner, on the junction of Clarkson Street and London Road, but the photographs for which he is best remembered are his views of Ipswich streets which provide a valuable record of changes to the Victorian town.

Some of his pictures purported to show an even earlier Ipswich, for one of the mounted prints which he sold 'at moderate prices', to quote his advertisement, bore the unlikely caption 'Old Butter Market and Queen Street, 1830'; the earliest-known paper negative dates from 1835. Vick appears to have traded very successfully on a wave of late-Victorian nostalgia, for the most popular of his mounted prints were those that showed buildings already demolished to make way for the Victorian buildings we today are only just beginning to appreciate.

Photographic printing was a somewhat time-consuming process in the third quarter of the nineteenth century, for the sensitized paper had to be placed behind the large glass plate in a wooden frame with a hinged back and exposed to sunlight for some considerable time. When the paper was sufficiently exposed (this could be ascertained by opening a hinged section of the wooden frame, since with printing-out paper the image appeared on the paper in increasing density as the exposure increased) it had to be removed from the frame and fixed in 'hypo' for two minutes. Then it had to be thoroughly washed to remove all traces of the chemical, clipped on to a line to dry, and finally mounted on the card on which it was sold.

Such a process proved unequal to the demand in the case of the more popular pictures, as only a single negative was likely to be available. Vick overcame the bottleneck by making a glass positive from the original negative and then using the positive to produce a number of copy negatives that could be used to produce contact prints for sale. With the most popular pictures of all there might be as many as a dozen copy negatives of the same view in use in his studio, as one can discover from the boxes of glass negatives now in the Suffolk Record Office.

A slightly later Ipswich photographer was Harry Walters, who is said to have made his first camera in the 1870s with the aid of bits and pieces such as a cardboard pillbox which he used as a lens holder. By the

An evocative picture of travelling people with a performing bear. In the last century there were many such itinerant performers, including Italian hurdy-gurdy men and German bands. There is a story of one such traveller who with a dancing bear boarded a Lowestoft tram; their appearance up the rear stairs was the cause of all the upper-deck passengers departing hurriedly down the front stairs. Left alone, the bear became bored, so his master brought out his concertina and the bear began to dance, a performance that caused consternation whenever the tram came to a stop; those waiting to board the tram all decided to wait for the next one. Subsequently the management issued an order that no bears were to be allowed to travel on the town's trams in future. (East Anglian Film Archive)

early years of the twentieth century he was in business at premises in Crown Street, Ipswich, from where he soon moved to a shop next to the Running Buck on St Margaret's Plain, where he remained until his death in 1926.

Harry Walters was an entertainer as well as a photographer, obviously a man with a keen sense of humour. Entertainment and photography became inextricably mixed when he indulged in his favourite trick photography, which included taking multiple pictures of himself. As Harry Wilmott, the negro comedian, he was well known on the local stage; when a plinth was erected in Christchurch Park for a statue of Queen Victoria he took a photograph of himself with his banjo standing on the plinth and entitled it 'Harry Wilmott as he appeared before the Queen' – before, that is, Queen Victoria's statue was installed.

It is impossible, of course, to go through the whole list of the county's early photographers. In Stowmarket there was Arthur Bugg, who operated from a small hut in Finborough Road, in Sudbury there were Miss Susanna Berry and Ambrose Copsey, in Haverhill Charles Mizon, and in Bury St Edmunds William Silas Spanton, John William Clarke and William Aston. Even quite small villages like Brockford and Hoxne had their photographers.

With the growing fashion for picture postcards at the beginning of this century it becomes less easy to assign photographs to particular photographers, though some like Fred Jenkins at Southwold and his brother Harry at Lowestoft took care to stamp their names on the cards they sold to holidaymakers and local people alike.

In an advertisement of 1904 the Southwold Jenkins advised amateur photographers, of whom there were by that time a great many, 'Do not send your PLATES and FILMS to an inexperienced Chemist for Development and Printing'; instead he suggested that they should bring them to one who made a speciality of the work. There is even a suggestion that he had a special darkroom for use by amateur photographers.

Charles Emeny and his son Clement at Felixstowe produced photographs of local scenes and local happenings over a period of some eighty years, for Charles was taking photographs as early as 1867, when he was a youngster of eighteen, and Clement retired only in 1950. When the Royal Naval Air Station was established at Felixstowe in 1913 Charles Emeny became friendly with some of the officers there, with the result that he was one of the earliest to take pictures from the air.

Yet all too many photographs cannot be ascribed to any particular man. Who was the photographer who cycled out to Long Melford in about 1912 to take photographs for reproduction as postcards, and left his cycle leaning against a lamp post as he took the pictures? Could it have been Frank Dicks, of 54 North Street, Sudbury, or Thomas Gates, of 1 Station Road, Sudbury? Or could it have been someone from Emeny & Sons, of 8 Gainsborough Street; and was this family any relation of Charles Emeny at Felixstowe?

When one writes a book one should be answering questions, not asking them, but sometimes one has to admit to not knowing the answer. Dating photographs is by no means easy, and there are many pitfalls. One can spend a considerable time searching with a magnifying glass for clues, and then be misled by a mistake in a directory that includes a particular shop long after it had closed, or fails to record a firm that was indeed trading at the time.

The author has made considerable efforts to date the photographs in this book, but having due regard to the perilous nature of the task apologizes in advance for errors the reader may discover.

For help in the compilation and writing of this book the author has to thank the staff of Suffolk Record Office, David Cleveland, Ivan Codd, the East Anglian Film Archive, Haverhill & District Local History Group, Hugh Moffat, Peter Northeast, John Wilton and others too numerous to mention individually who have been generous with information and with the loan of photographs. Those pictures not otherwise acknowledged are from the author's collection; he is mindful that many of these were given to him in the distant past by friends.

THE WAVENEY VALLEY

The impressive walls and bastions of Burgh Castle (now in Norfolk, but until 1974 a part of Suffolk) remain as one of the most outstanding monuments of Roman occupation. This photograph by George Christopher Davies, an amateur photographer and Broads sailor who did much to put the area on the tourist map, dates from c. 1880. When the fort was built in the second half of the third century it faced out on to a broad estuary with a substantial Roman port on the north side at Caister-by-Yarmouth.

The broads were formed in medieval times as peat pits, from which fuel was obtained both for the local salt industry and for monastic establishments such as the cathedral priory at Norwich. Fritton Lake was one of those formed in side valleys rather than in the marshes alongside the main rivers and was later used as a duck decoy for capturing wild ducks for the table. An average take each season was about a thousand ducks. This photograph showing the mouth of the decoy pipe is, like the others on succeeding pages, from a series of sixteen negatives taken by G.C. Davies in 1882. As Davies and his companions approached the decoy on their first visit they were given a piece of smouldering turf to carry, the object being to destroy their own scent which would have alarmed the ducks.

The decoyman and the decoy dog, whose job was to arouse the ducks' curiosity and attract them into the pipe, standing by the purse net at the end of the pipe. When the ducks reached this end of the net they were doomed; their necks would be wrung so silently by the decoyman that their fellows outside the pipe would remain unaware of the danger.

Reed screens at the side of the pipe were so angled that seen from the lake they presented a solid wall. The low walls seen in the lower picture were termed 'dog jumps'; the decoy dog would leap over one and disappear, luring the curious ducks further up the pipe towards the fatal purse net at the end.

A cargo-carrying billy-boy on its way upriver to Beccles passes a group of yachts belonging to members of the Yare Sailing Club near the entrance to Oulton Dyke on 3 August 1881. For many years Beccles was a minor inland port, importing grain and coal and exporting malt and flour; there was a short-lived revival of trade in the 1950s when Thames barges brought wheat to Green's mills in the town.

The same billy-boy lying at Beccles Quay a day or two later, seen in another of G.C. Davies' photographs.
A new bridge was under construction at the time to replace the stone one that had existed since at least
the early seventeenth century, and the building operations can be seen in the background.

Three wherries, one of them either newly built or just refitted, lie above the bridge in this view of Beccles from the river, *c.* 1881. Seagoing vessels could not pass under the bridge, but wherries went on upriver to Bungay through a series of locks.

Boater's Hills, seen in a photograph taken *c.* 1904, were at one time a favourite pleasure resort of the people of Beccles. This pleasant spot on the Norfolk bank of the Waveney a mile or so below the town took its name from a boathouse which stood on the riverside; the word boat'us, as pronounced locally, became corrupted to Boater's.

Little groups of men find time for a mardle (local term for a chat) on the corner of Market Street and Smallgate, Beccles, in the early 1920s. Prominent in this view is the stationery shop of Harry Webster, who published a postcard of the scene. Webster had taken over the business carried on for many years by Caleb Chase. On the other side of Smallgate is the White Lion Hotel, which at this time still advertised itself as a posting house; horses could be hired there.

The church of St Michael's at Beccles is unusual in having a detached tower standing near the east end. When construction of the tower began in the early sixteenth century it was obviously considered unsafe to build at the west end of the church since so massive a structure might prove unstable at the top of the steep slope down to Pudding Moor. Impressive as it is, the tower was never completed; there should have been another stage above what is now the top stage.

Beccles post office in Exchange Square, looking down Smallgate to the stuccoed frontage of the Public Hall at the top of Station Road. Below is a view of Pudding Moor, a street which runs parallel with the River Waveney at the foot of a steep slope down from the town. In this case Moor is equated with marsh rather than heather-clad upland, and Pudding is the local name for a toad.

The Market Place at Bungay, with the tower of St Mary's Church rising above the rooftops. Like its neighbour Beccles, Bungay suffered a severe fire in the seventeenth century and almost all the older buildings were erected following the destruction wrought by the fire. It was at that time that the handsome Butter Cross was erected in the Market Place. On the left of the picture, taken in the 1920s, is the grocer's shop of Brewster & Balls, who as can be seen were also wine and spirit merchants. This picture, taken by a photographer employed by Jarrolds of Norwich, was used to produce a postcard sold by H.W. Short, printer, stationer, bookbinder, bookseller and newsagent at 14 Market Place.

The lead figure of Justice, holding a sword in her right hand and scales in her left, was added to the Butter Cross in 1754. The Direct Meat Supply Company in the shop behind the cross advertises 'Best English Mutton' in an advertisement that has apparently been painted on the wall since the date of the picture on the opposite page.

St Mary's Church, Bungay, is now the town's principal church. This 1920s photograph, reproduced on another of H.W. Short's postcards, shows the then-new town war memorial, bearing the names of 102 Bungay men who died in the First World War. Attached to St Mary's was at one time the church of the Holy Cross, used by the Benedictine nunnery. The nunnery buildings were destroyed in the 1668 fire.

Bridge Street, Bungay, naturally takes its name from the bridge linking Bungay and Ditchingham across the Waveney, which here makes a great loop around Bungay Common. Below is Bungay's second parish church, Holy Trinity, with its eleventh-century round tower.

The big tower mill at Bungay, built in 1830. In the days when windmills ground much of the grain grown on Suffolk farms Bungay had several mills, including a postmill that stood quite close to this one.

Staithe Road which, as its name implies, led to Bungay Staithe, the head of navigation on the Waveney. To reach the staithe, wherries had to negotiate locks at Shipmeadow, Ellingham and Wainford, provided under an Act of Parliament of 1670. The last company to operate the navigation were the local millers and maltsters, W.D. & A.E. Walker, who built some of their own wherries at the staithe. No wherries have come to Bungay since 1934, when the navigation closed.

The wherry *Albion* at Bungay Staithe, *c.* 1900. Although often referred to as 'a Norfolk wherry', the *Albion* was built by Billy Brighton at Oulton Broad and was owned by W.D. & A.E. Walker, so she most definitely belonged to Suffolk.

Skinner's Mill at Stradbroke bore the date 1688 on part of its structure, though it had clearly been rebuilt and updated more than once since its original erection. The patent sails, invented by William Cubitt, who became consulting engineer to Ransomes at Ipswich, and the fantail that kept the mill into wind were nineteenth-century improvements.

The little town of Eye was until local government reorganization in 1974 a self-governing borough with mayor and corporation. Only horse-drawn vehicles are to be seen in this photograph, probably taken *c.* 1912, the youthful driver of the cart in the right foreground being dressed in schoolboy attire of the period. To the left are the shop of John Crisp, saddler, and the Horse Shoes Hotel, whose flaking sign announces it to be a posting establishment. On the opposite side of the street is the shop of Archibald Tipple, boot and shoe maker; Mrs May Tipple, possibly his wife, was about this time recorded as carrying on the trade of stocking knitter.

Schoolchildren, in this case girls, also appear in this photograph of Church Street, Eye, also from the pre-1914 period. The magnificent tower of SS Peter and Paul's Church, which provided a pattern for other parishes to aspire to, dominates the end of the street; wills of the 1450s and 1460s provide evidence of the building activities then going on, and there is a reference to the completion of the tower in 1470. It is said to have been financed 'partly with the plowgh, partly in churchales, partly in legacies given that waye, but chiefly of the frank & devowte hartes of the people'. To the left of the church is the early sixteenth-century Guildhall and on the right is the Eight Bells, kept in the early 1900s by Arthur Read.

In the early nineteenth century the castle hill at Eye was crowned by a post windmill, but this was replaced by the building shown in this view. The shape of the castle bailey laid out by William Malet to the west of the motte can still be seen reflected in the layout of the streets.

THE COAST & HEATHS

Victorian railway builder Samuel Morton Peto, later to be honoured with a baronetcy for his work in constructing a railway in the Crimea to carry supplies to the front, acquired Somerleyton Hall in 1844. On the foundations of the Elizabethan hall he built a Jacobean-style house, and in place of the existing village he built 'cottage-residences of a highly ornamental character' far superior to those occupied by most Victorian workers. His architect was the remarkable John Thomas, whose sculpture adorns the Houses of Parliament.

The main street of Corton, seen above in Edwardian times, bends abruptly to the left at its northern end, though doubtless it once continued on beyond where a cliff marks the present limit of the sea's advance. Much of the Suffolk coast has suffered from erosion, the most spectacular instance being the disappearance of the once-great seaport town of Dunwich which was already battling with the waves in the thirteenth century. Inland lies an area of what was once heathland, known today as the Sandlings. Almost all the heath has been lost to agriculture, to airfields, to forestry or to natural progression, though attempts are being made to save the last remnants by sheep grazing. Natural progression means the progression from heathland to scrubland when birches and thornbushes seed. When the heath was grazed by sheep this kind of vegetation was grazed off and could not get a hold, but without grazing it quite quickly takes over.

There have been coastal lights at Lowestoft since two leading lights were erected in 1609 to bring ships in through the Stanford Channel. The lighthouse seen in this picture of *c.* 1912 was erected in 1873–4 to replace the one built in 1676 at a time when Samuel Pepys was Master of Trinity House.

A series of narrow paths known as scores connect the town of Lowestoft with the Beach, that area of low-lying land below the cliff. In this view of Crown Score *c.* 1910 the Low Light can be seen standing near the water's edge.

A community of fishermen and other seafarers grew up on the Beach during the nineteenth century, and to serve this community Christ Church was built in 1868, two years after a separate ecclesiastical parish had been formed. When this photograph was taken *c.* 1910 as one of a series of postcards for Herbert George Rogers, a newsagent in London Road North, the Beach formed a thriving suburb with its own shops, pubs and institutions; in the 1960s it was cleared to become an industrial estate.

The South Pier which sheltered the outer harbour, built in mid-century by Morton Peto, was also the resort of holidaymakers. This part of Lowestoft became popular after Peto's development of a 'new town' on land south of the bridge, with terraces of brick-built houses designed by sculptor-architect John Thomas. The iron-framed Pier Pavilion seen in this 1890s photograph was opened in 1891 and survived until after the Second World War.

A notice warning that it is dangerous for children to play on the breakwater seems superfluous in these conditions. Seas such as these were responsible for the destruction of Will Edwards' concert hall on the South Beach on 11 September 1912, as seen below in a photograph by C.T. Metcalf, of London Road South, Lowestoft.

Inland from Lowestoft lies Oulton Broad, the most southerly of what are usually called 'the Norfolk Broads'. When Lowestoft harbour was constructed in the 1830s, as part of a scheme to bring seagoing vessels to Norwich, Oulton Broad and Lake Lothing were separated by a lock; the easterly section of Lake Lothing became the inner harbour, and the lock marked the division between salt water and fresh. The broad is linked with the Waveney by Oulton Dyke, which was widened and deepened to enable seagoing ships to pass through on their way to Norwich and Beccles. Today only pleasure craft are to be seen using the dyke.

To the south of Lowestoft lies the fishing village of Pakefield, a community that has suffered much from attacks by the sea. In between is Kirkley, which merged indefinably into Lowestoft as development proceeded during the nineteenth century and in 1907 became part of the borough of Lowestoft. Almost on the boundary with Pakefield is South Cliff Congregational Church, built at the beginning of the twentieth century on land given by James Jeremiah Colman, the mustard manufacturer; the church was quite new when this photograph was taken.

Kessingland was at one time reckoned to be the most prosperous village in Suffolk as a result of its participation in the herring fishing, and some of the beating chambers in which herring nets were repaired can still be seen there. Steam drifters were owned in Kessingland, and indeed the first steam drifter launched in Lowestoft in 1897, the year of Queen Victoria's diamond jubilee, was built for a Kessingland owner, but they worked from Lowestoft harbour. St Edmund's Church, with its lofty fifteenth-century tower, stands as evidence of an earlier prosperity no doubt based on coastal trade and fisheries.

For fifty years, from 1879 to 1929, the narrow-gauge Southwold Railway operated from Halesworth to Southwold. Local legend tells how the rolling stock was brought back from China after the closure of the pioneering Shanghai and Woosung line, but in fact the gauge was different and the Southwold engines were built by Sharp, Stewart in Manchester especially for the Southwold Railway. In fact it was the engine driver who had returned from China, for a Mr W.G. Jackson who had driven the first train on the Woosung tramway became the Southwold Railway's first locomotive foreman. The picture, from the beginning of the twentieth century, shows no. 1 *Southwold* in Southwold station.

Fishermen's sheds on the beach at Southwold in the 1880s. In the middle of the picture is a ramshackle shed that shows signs of having been originally roofed with an upturned boat, probably a fishing punt like those lying on the shingle.

A special occasion in Southwold Market Place, *c.* 1909. Unfortunately the reason for the gathering is not known, but it is typical of Southwold that any special event should be attended by such a considerable crowd. The town had a long history of self-government, but the mayor and members of the corporation are not in evidence on this occasion.

St Edmund's Church, Southwold, seen in the late nineteenth century. The church, with its superlative tower, was built in the decades between 1430 and 1460 when the Wars of the Roses were bringing havoc to the kingdom, which perhaps makes the achievement of the builders even more magnificent. Sir Nikolaus Pevsner calls St Edmund's 'the epitome of Suffolk flushwork'.

A photograph from the 1880s of the ferryman who operated the ferry from Southwold to Walberswick sitting in the ferry boat on the Walberswick side. It seems that the ferry was an ancient one, since there is a mention of a ferry boat in the thirteenth century.

In 1885 the River Blyth Ferry Company was formed to provide a chain ferry to carry vehicles across the river, and the original hand-cranked ferry was later replaced by one powered by steam. In this picture from early in the twentieth century a horse-drawn carriage is about to be taken over to Southwold.

Walberswick Church, seen here in a photograph from a Victorian album, fell into decay when the village of Walberswick itself declined in importance and the parishioners became unable to keep such a large building in repair. Most unusually, we do know the names of those responsible for building the fine tower, since in an agreement of 1425 which survives they are named as 'Richard Russel of Dunwich and Adam Powle of Blythburgh'.

The River Blyth was made navigable up to the market town of Halesworth in the 1750s, and for more than a century keels and then wherries fetched by sea from the Broads rivers carried coal and other goods up to the quay seen in the picture above. The Thoroughfare, seen below at a time of celebration in the early years of the twentieth century, is the commercial heart of Halesworth.

Henham Hall, the home of the Earls of Stradbroke, was built in 1793 by James Wyatt, twenty years after its Elizabethan predecessor had been destroyed by fire. Edward Barry 'beautified' it in the nineteenth century, but the hall was demolished in 1953. Below is a shoot on the Henham estate in Victorian times.

The town of Dunwich was a thriving seaport in the early Middle Ages, but storms blocked its harbour and submerged its streets, eventually swallowing up almost every building. The last of its eight, or possibly nine, churches to survive the onslaught was All Saints', seen here as a nineteenth-century ruin. A series of picture postcards published in the twentieth century show it gradually slipping down the cliff as storms ate their way into the land; all is now gone, and the cliff line has reached the western, landward ramparts of the medieval town.

Kelsale lies just to the east of the old Little Yarmouth Turnpike, the main road from Ipswich to Lowestoft and Yarmouth. The guildhall, seen in the 1900-ish picture above, was built in about 1495 and restored in the nineteenth century for use as a parochial school. A couple of miles to the south the main road passed through the middle of Saxmundham, diving under the East Suffolk line railway bridge, seen below *c.* 1920.

Aldeburgh beach and the town's two lifeboats in the early years of the twentieth century. The nearer boat is the no. 1 boat *City of Winchester*, with the no. 2 boat *Edward Z. Dresden* beyond. The former boat was built to replace the ill-fated *Aldeburgh* which capsized on 7 December 1899, with the loss of six of her crew of eighteen. Up to the time of the disaster the *Aldeburgh* had been launched on service fifty-four times, and had saved 152 lives. A later Aldeburgh lifeboat, the motor lifeboat *Abdy Beauclerk*, carried out the first war service of any lifeboat in the British Isles during the Second World War when she went out to the Brocklebank liner *Magdapur* which had been sunk by a magnetic mine just a week after the outbreak of war in 1939.

The former fishing smack *Ionia*, converted to a houseboat, was a feature of the River Alde at Aldeburgh for more than half a century. A fleet of cod smacks once worked out of Aldeburgh, but the *Ionia* was not one of them; she had been a Grimsby trawling smack working from the Humber.

Opposite. Snape windmill, which was dismantled in the 1930s. The brick roundhouse was converted into a house and was used by Benjamin Britten when composing some of his music.

Framlingham is a small town that owed its early importance to the castle established by Roger Bigod on land given to him *c.* 1100 by Henry I. In later days 'Fram' was the centre of an agricultural area well known for dairying. Gostling & Company had this chemist's shop on the Market Hill at Framlingham at the beginning of the twentieth century, and from the evidence of the bills on display in the photograph they were much involved in veterinary medicines. Herbert Sara seems to have taken over the business *c.* 1914.

A flourishing port on the River Deben, Woodbridge was in the nineteenth century a busy place with many maltings, mills, a shipyard and an iron foundry. The junction of Cumberland Street, to the left in the above picture, the Thoroughfare, to the right, and Church Street, straight ahead, is known as Cross Corner, from The Cross public house, said on the sign to have been established in 1652; the public house probably took its name from the crossroads in the first place. The photographer is unknown, but the postcard was published by George Booth, printer and stationer in Church Street. At the mouth of the Deben is Felixstowe Ferry, seen in the picture below looking across the river to Bawdsey.

Prominent in this photograph of Felixstowe beach, taken in the summer of 1889, is Charles Emeny's photographic studio. Charles Emeny and his son Clement chronicled the development of the town, which became a popular resort after the Empress of Germany, a daughter of Queen Victoria, chose to bring her

family to the town for a seaside holiday in 1891 while the Emperor was carrying out his official duties on a visit to Britain. The tower of South Beach Mansion, where the Empress stayed, can be seen above the row of buildings in the right background. (David Cleveland)

Among the Victorian businessmen from Ipswich who acquired summer homes in Felixstowe and Walton, the older settlement lying just inland from the new resort, was Richard Dykes Alexander. This early photograph, probably taken by Alexander himself, shows the Alexanders at Lavender Cottage, Walton, in the 1860s. So long was the usual exposure that it was possible for the photographer to put himself in the picture. (Suffolk Record Office)

IPSWICH & AROUND

At the bottom of Bourne Hill, on the approach to Ipswich from the Manningtree direction, stands the Wherstead Ostrich, a hostelry that is said to have been built in 1612. The sign of the Ostrich, a bird of that kind with a horseshoe in its beak, was taken from the crest of Sir Edward Coke, the seventeenth-century Chief Justice, who acquired the manor of Bourne Hall, on whose lands the inn was built, in 1609. In 1996 the name was changed to The Oyster Reach, lending credence to an historical misapprehension that attributed the name to nearby oyster layings in the Orwell. (Hugh Moffat)

Pond Hall Farm on the Ipswich side of the Orwell some distance below the town, seen *c*. 1900 in a photograph taken by Alexander Moffat, an amateur photographer who became town clerk of Ipswich. The photograph of the Ostrich on the previous page was also taken by him. Near Pond Hall at John's Ness the Ipswich shipbuilder John Barnard built the Fourth Rate *Hampshire* of fifty guns in 1741. (Hugh Moffat)

Almost opposite Pond Hall stands Freston Tower, an enigmatic Tudor tower in diapered red brickwork standing in parkland sloping up from the river, here seen in a photograph from a Victorian album. Tradition associates the tower with the Latimers, but it was probably built by a prominent Ipswich merchant, Thomas Gooding, who succeeded the Latimers at Freston. There are many legends connected with the tower, but they are just that, legends.

Gainsborough Lane, on the eastern outskirts of Ipswich, was a favourite with photographers and postcard publishers at the beginning of the twentieth century. Today the land is covered with council houses. In the picture below harvesters are at work in the field not many miles from the centre of Ipswich.

As the town expanded houses were built on the town rampart surrounding the medieval core of Ipswich. These houses in Tower Ramparts survived well into the twentieth century, but both the houses and the rampart have disappeared since the photograph was taken.

Above is Upper Brook Street, Ipswich, *c.* 1885, with the shops at the end of the Buttermarket projecting in the background. The road was widened there in the 1930s. In the Buttermarket is the Ancient House, seen on the opposite page in the 1890s when Fred Pawsey was occupying it as a bookshop and stationer. It is apparent that even a hundred years ago tourists were coming to Ipswich, to judge from the advertisement in the window. The pargeting on the walls of the Ancient House dates from *c.* 1670, whereas the house itself is older.

Richard Dykes Alexander took this photograph of the cottage occupied by 'the keeper of the Promenade' in the 1860s. The Promenade was an avenue alongside the New Cut which used to be a favourite resort of Ipswich people, and the cottage stood roughly where the entrance to the Wet Dock is now. (Suffolk Record Office)

Another early photograph by Richard Dykes Alexander shows the Umbrella shelter at the end of the Promenade. Although the Promenade was lost to Ipswich as a result of dock expansion between the two world wars the Umbrella survived in a state of increasing dilapidation into the 1950s. (Suffolk Record Office)

When the Ipswich Ragged School attempted in 1849 to provide some kind of education for children 'too ragged, too filthy, too ignorant, for ordinary instruction' it was Richard Dykes Alexander who provided the money to pay for the school's operations. The children were taught to be self-sufficient, and to that end (in this photograph by Alexander) the master, Joshua Newman, is superintending them in cutting and bundling firewood. No doubt the sales of the bundles helped to pay for the day-to-day work of the school. (Suffolk Record Office)

Robert Burrows, an Ipswich artist turned photographer, took this photograph of a barquentine at Ipswich in 1858. He seems to have had a particular interest in the local shipping, for he took many pictures in and around the Wet Dock, which when opened in 1842 was the biggest of its kind in the country, much larger than any dock on the Thames or at Hull or Liverpool. (Suffolk Record Office)

Overleaf. The Ipswich Lifeboat Saturday procession passing over Cornhill on 10 July 1897, taken by Alexander Moffat. The background to the picture is provided by T.W. Cotman's distinctive façade of 1889. (Hugh Moffat)

Looking west along Tavern Street in the 1880s. Prominent on the right of this photograph by William Vick are the premises of Lewis Brothers, linen drapers and silk mercers, who declared in an advertisement that their black silks 'have been sent to all parts of England, Scotland, to the Continent of Europe, and to the English Colonies'. By the 1890s the Lewises had been succeeded by Sydney William Cook, who carried on the same trade for several more years before the premises were taken over by the Capital & Counties Bank.

In 1867 the old town hall was replaced by an imposing building 'in the Venetian style', which was in 1881 joined by an almost equally imposing head post office. Cornhill had, as its name suggests, originally been the site of the corn market, and it was for many years until 1812 used for the sale of cattle. At one side of Cornhill stood St Mildred's Church, which became redundant in the Middle Ages and was converted into a town hall; the last traces of the former church were removed when the old town hall was demolished for the building of the new. In the same way the Corn Exchange which had in 1812 taken the place of a strange building called the Rotunda itself gave way to the new post office building in 1880–1, a new Corn Exchange then being erected behind the town hall.

As the town expanded during the nineteenth century many Ipswich landmarks disappeared. One of them was the Brook's Hall pond, seen here in a photograph of 1869, another of those issued by William Vick although it is possible it was taken by his predecessor William Cobb. The pond was filled in when houses spread along Norwich Road. Note the loose surface of what was then the main road to Stowmarket, Bury St Edmunds and Norwich.

CENTRAL SUFFOLK

Encapsulated within Sir Charles Barry's Italianate mansion at Shrubland, 5 miles north of Ipswich, is the eighteenth-century hall built by James Paine for the Rev. John Bacon. The gardens were modelled by Barry on those of the Villa d'Este at Tivoli. Today Shrubland attracts those who can afford to seek their health expensively and looks down on the roaring traffic of the A14 trunk road.

Sir Charles Barry's gardens were altered later in the nineteenth century by William Robinson, creator of the English herbaceous border. Coddenham Lodge, below, on the eastern side of Shrubland Park, still appears to have been transplanted from Tuscany.

The unusual weatherboarded top stage of the tower distinguishes the church of St Mary and St Lambert, Stonham Aspal. It was added in the eighteenth century by Squire Theodore Eccleston, who was so keen a bellringer that he substituted a ring of ten for the original five bells and needed an extra-large bell chamber to house them. The Bullnose Morris bears an East Sussex registration; did it perhaps belong to the unknown photographer? In the churchyard is a monument to the Revd Anthony Wingfield which, says Sir Nikolaus Pevsner, 'is so unlike anything one is used to in churchyards that one feels a monument in Westminster Abbey may be taking a country holiday'.

The Magpie at Stonham Parva, known to travellers of a bygone age as 'Stonham Pie', once had a live magpie in the cage to be seen on the front wall beside the door. It also possessed a sign spanning the Norwich road, a Roman road known as the Pye Road from which it got its name. In spite of the great increase in traffic it still retains its sign across the road, but the cage no longer contains a live bird.

Every Suffolk town has its story of disaster by fire, some being almost totally destroyed as the flames leapt from building to building and street to street, fanned by a fresh breeze. It was on a Sunday morning in July 1868 that fire broke out in Bury Street, Stowmarket, and no fewer than eighty-one people were made homeless. (Ivan Codd)

Although in the nineteenth century Stowmarket became a minor industrial centre with an agricultural engineering works and foundry, an artificial fertilizer factory and even an explosives works, it continued to play its traditional role as a market town midway between Ipswich and Bury St Edmunds. This view of the market, held in the triangular Market Place, dates from the early 1920s; later in the decade Samuel Pluck's outfitter's shop and boot store became the National Provincial Bank, and Pluck retreated to his other store in Station Road. (Ivan Codd)

Overleaf. All over the country people celebrated Queen Victoria's Diamond Jubilee in 1897. Here the crowds gather in the Market Place at Stowmarket for the celebrations, with the men of Combs Brass Band in their smart uniforms ready to provide music for the occasion. (Ivan Codd)

For a few years just before the outbreak of the First World War Charles Miller had a hardware store in Regent Street, Stowmarket, and a horse-drawn cart in which he hawked his wares around the surrounding villages. Along with his pots and pans he sold woven wire covers to keep the flies off the cold joint, and also Lipton's tea. Many small communities depended on such traders for household articles, for a trip to the nearest market town was by no means an everyday occurrence. (Ivan Codd)

A view of Ipswich Street, Stowmarket, in the early years of the twentieth century, with the Duke's Head on the left and the tower and spire of the parish church of St Peter and St Mary looming in the background. Until the construction of the Gipping Valley bypass in quite recent years this was part of the main road between Ipswich, Bury St Edmunds and Cambridge, yet traffic is so slight that youngsters have no fears about posing in the middle of the street for the photographer. The Duke's Head still exists, but the rest of the scene has changed dramatically as the result of redevelopment. (Ivan Codd)

The Prentice family began producing artificial manure at Stowmarket in 1856, and in the following decade branched out into the manufacture of guncotton. The manufacturing process was far from safe, and in 1864 two women employees died in an explosion; a much more devastating series of explosions occurred in 1871, resulting in the deaths of twenty-four people and widespread damage to the town. Above is a view of the rebuilt works on the River Gipping, c. 1900. (Ivan Codd)

A march undertaken by strikers from the explosives works during a long-lasting dispute with the New Explosives Company in 1913; they are making their way along Ipswich Street. In spite of increasing hardship in the town the strikers held out for an increase in local wages that were below those paid in the industry elsewhere. (Ivan Codd)

Overleaf. The absence of traffic is noticeable in this view of Bury Street, Stowmarket, looking up from the Tavern Street junction. The juxtaposition of William Huble Druce's haircutting, shaving and shampooing establishment and the cycle shop of T.H. Nice & Company, with its Michelin advertisements, dates the photograph to *c.* 1906. (Ivan Codd)

Travelling showmen had their fixed times for visiting different places, often based on the dates of the old trading or hiring fairs of earlier centuries. At Stowmarket they were still using the Dukes Head Meadow in Temple Road, off Ipswich Street, in the 1920s, by which time motor caravans were taking over from the traditional horse-drawn caravans of earlier days. The Regal cinema was built on the site in 1936 and the showmen had to find another setting for the fair. (Ivan Codd)

Opposite. The Deanery Tower at Hadleigh, completed *c.* 1495, was built by William Pykenham, Archdeacon of Suffolk, who was appointed rector of Hadleigh in 1472. It is generally supposed that the tower was to have been the gatehouse to a palace whose building was brought to an end by Pykenham's death in 1497. Besides being a fine example of fifteenth-century brickwork the Deanery Tower has its place in ecclesiastical history as the setting for a conference in 1833 which gave rise to the Oxford Movement.

Two views of Hadleigh High Street in the days when traffic was horse drawn and was limited to the occasional waggon or cart. On the right of the picture above can be seen the Coffee Tavern at 66 High Street, established *c.* 1890 in an attempt to break the attraction of the public houses; it was in being for around half a century, and the name is still used for the end shop of this seventeenth-century block. The lower picture, looking in the opposite direction, shows the White Lion Hotel and a building with a pargetted upper storey which fortunately survives. In both pictures it is possible to see water running in the deep gutters; in spite of a petition presented to the Local Board in 1881 by High Street residents complaining of 'the stench which arises from this gutter in consequence of its being used as a drain', the water continued to run until well within living memory.

The original part of Hadleigh Guildhall, the central double-jettied section in this view, dates back to the mid-fifteenth century when it served as a market house. The market rights were granted to the lord of the manor of Toppesfield Manor in 1252 and were transferred by William de Clopton to fifteen trustees in 1438; the successors to those trustees, the Hadleigh Market Feoffment, still operate the Guildhall and have in recent years spent a large amount on its restoration. The building has in its time been used as a school, as a workhouse and as the town hall, a new town hall being built on to the old Guildhall in the nineteenth century.

The village of Brettenham lies some 7 miles to the west of Stowmarket. The little River Brett rises in the parish and makes its way through Chelsworth and Hadleigh to its confluence with the Stour near Higham. The name of the village is thought to be derived from Bretta's ham or home, Bretta possibly being 'the Briton'; the river name is a back-formation from the village. In about 1830 Joseph Bonaparte, brother of Napoleon and ex-king of Naples and of Spain, lived at Brettenham Hall, which in later years when it was the residence of Sir Thomas Courtenay Theydon Warner MP was surrounded by somewhat fabulous gardens. The hall is now a school. (John Wilton)

THE STOUR VALLEY

The lower part of the Stour is well known as Constable Country, while the upper section towards Sudbury is forever linked with Thomas Gainsborough, who was the son of a Sudbury weaver. John Constable's father operated Flatford Mill and young John learned his trade as a miller. All the elements that John said made him an artist are seen in this view of Flatford taken on a glass plate negative by an unknown turn-of-the-century photographer.

John Constable produced a number of sketches and paintings of St Mary's Church in his native village of East Bergholt. This photograph, printed from a glass plate exposed by an unknown photographer *c*. 1900, shows the church very much as the artist knew it, though the interior was considerably altered by the Victorians. An early Constable drawing shows the chancel interior with a substantial gallery spanning the chancel arch and box pews almost hiding the Laudian altar rails, replaced later by telescopic brass rails.

The tower of East Bergholt church was never completed because the Reformation brought an end to bequests to such building projects, so the ring of bells is in a bell cage in the churchyard. Instead of being operated by bell-ropes from below the bells have to be swung by hand by ringers standing on the bell frame.

A view of Flatford Mill, once operated by John Constable's father, Golding Constable, seen from the Essex side of the river. Flour produced at the mill was taken downstream by lighters and transhipped at Mistley Quay into seagoing vessels, including Golding Constable's *Telegraph*, for onward carriage to London. Just above the mill was a dry dock in which the river lighters were built and repaired, as seen in Constable's sketch of boatbuilding, Flatford, dated 7 September 1814, and the painting exhibited at the Royal Academy the following year.

Dedham Vale is known as the Constable Country, and to those who know his pictures well reminders of the artist are everywhere to be seen. This picture of Stoke-by-Nayland Church, printed from a glass plate negative of *c*. 1900, shows a scene almost identical to that sketched by Constable in 1814, except that the little building on the left does not appear in the drawing.

Edward Baker's mills at Great Cornard were originally powered only by the water of the River Stour, which also served to carry the flour they produced on its way to London. The arrival of steam power enabled Baker to expand his mills, and towards the end of the nineteenth century the old millstones were replaced by roller mills introduced by Suffolk millwrights from eastern Europe.

At the beginning of the twentieth century the village of Great Cornard, on the Suffolk side of the Stour little more than a mile from Sudbury, had a population of fewer than a thousand. The scattered village whose centre is seen in the photograph above has been expanded since the Second World War by the building of large estates by the Greater London Council to house those who sought to escape from the Metropolis.

The tower of All Saints' Church, Sudbury, is prominent in this view across the old timber Ballingdon Bridge in the early years of the twentieth century. Sudbury is a very ancient town with a history of cloth manufacture; although production of woollen cloth ceased many years ago it still has several silk mills. The timber bridge seen here was later replaced by a new bridge in more modern materials. (John Wilton)

There is a story that bull baiting used to be one of the attractions at the Bull Inn, Sudbury, seen here with the tower of All Saints' Church looming over it. The building dates from the middle of the sixteenth century and the main door, made of oak plank, used to have the date 1694 scratched on it. It is no longer a public house, having lost its licence in the 1950s.

Stour Street contains fine timber-framed houses and was once inhabited by some of the town's more affluent residents. In the picture above we are looking out of town towards Cross Street, and in the one below we are looking back towards Gainsborough Street, on the corner of which are the premises of Ebenezer Hitchcock, cooper (a maker of barrels); on the wall he advertises also 'creamery and dairy', so it seems that like many old-time tradesmen he had several strings to his bow.

Cross Street is one of Sudbury's oldest streets, described by Celia Fiennes in 1689 as an 'aristocratic suburb'. On the right is a fifteenth-century house long known as 'Ye Old Moot Hall'; the Moot Hall was in fact on the Market Hill, but this building might at one time have been a guildhall. In the 1890s a woman photographer, Miss Susanna Berry, was working from 78 Cross Street. Since this photograph was taken, *c.* 1912, some of the buildings have been cleared away and replaced; indeed after the Second World War a report recommended the eradication of the whole area, which had gained a poor reputation, but wiser counsels have since prevailed.

On 1 October 1929 the civic pride of the Borough of Sudbury is blossoming, and hundreds throng Market Hill to watch the proceedings. The United States Ambassador, General Charles Gates Dawes, whose ancestor William Dawes sailed in the ship *Planter* to settle in the New World, is to be admitted an Honorary Freeman of the borough. In the picture opposite the mayor, Edward Page FitzGerald, presents General Dawes with an illuminated scroll recording the council's resolution to grant him the honorary freedom. (East Anglian Film Archive)

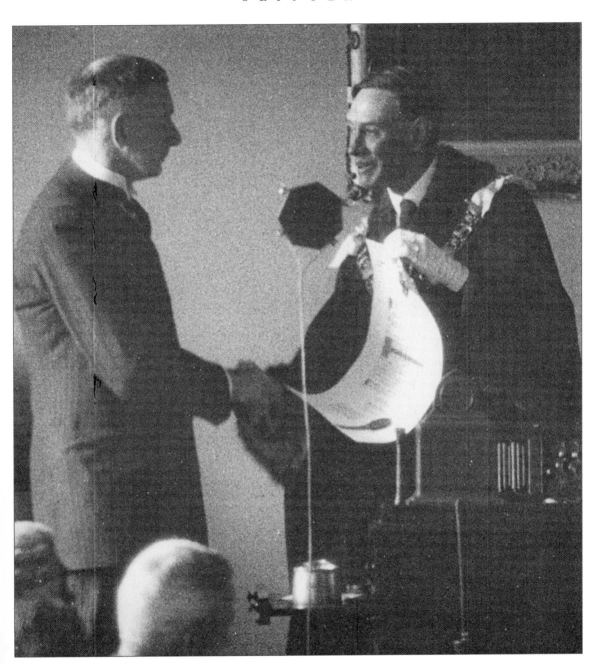

Today, in spite of the opening of a bypass, traffic pours through Long Melford's main street in an almost continuous stream. In this view of Hall Street at the beginning of the twentieth century there is no sign of any traffic whatever, unless one includes cattle only loosely controlled by a boy with a stout stick. Are they perhaps heading for the slaughterhouse behind Alfred Allen's butcher's shop on the right-hand side, with its blind extended to keep the sun off the meat?

The photographer's bicycle leans against a lamp post, his heavy leather case strapped to the carrier, while he sets up this shot of Melford Green, with Holy Trinity Church and Trinity Hospital at the head of the green. The church is one of the finest in Suffolk, but the tower which seems to complement the building so well is, surprisingly, a modern rebuilding. The original was lost in a fire, and the replacement built early in the eighteenth century was somewhat lacking in stature; it was 'restored' by George F. Bodley between 1900 and 1904 to match the scale and character of the rest of the church, the new tower encasing the eighteenth-century one.

The photographer's bicycle appears again in this picture of the gate to Melford Hall, home of the Hyde Parker family. Before the Dissolution of the Monasteries the hall belonged to the abbots of Bury St Edmunds, and some time in the middle of the sixteenth century it was acquired from Henry VIII by lawyer Sir William Cordell, one of those people who was able to survive changes of monarch and of religion in that difficult period. In 1578 his fortune, made through his legal career, was put to the test when he entertained Queen Elizabeth I at Melford. We are told that 'there was in Suffolke suche sumptuous feastinges and bankets as seldom in anie parte of the worlde there hath been seene afore. The Maister of the Rolles, Sir William Cordell, was the first that bganne this greate feasting at his house of Melforde, and did lyght such a candle to the rest of the shire, that they were gladd bountifullie and francklie to followe the same example.' Some fortunes were consumed in the flame of that candle, but not Sir William's.

The name Melford is said to be derived from the mill ford. In this photograph the site of the ford can be seen as well as the weatherboarded building of the Hall Mill, one of three corn mills that once existed in Long Melford. In the foreground is one of the gas lamps supplied by the local gasworks, at one time owned by the local ironfounders, Ward & Silver, and later by the Long Melford Gas Co. Ltd.

Lavenham is visited by thousands of tourists every year because it has retained so many of its fine timber-framed buildings, but it is by no means as unchanging as many of the visitors imagine. Above is a photograph taken by F. Lingard Ranson, Lavenham photographer and historian, of the old post office on the corner of High Street and Hall Lane, probably just before or just after the First World War. The next-door building, now known as The Crooked House, has a nineteenth-century frontage to the ground floor; in the later picture on the opposite page the nineteenth-century brickwork and sash windows have been replaced by a timber-framed wall with leaded windows in the position of the Tudor original.

The well-known Swan Hotel at Lavenham, standing at the junction of High Street and Water Street (so called from the stream which still flows beneath ground), was at one time a coaching inn. The old coach entrance can be seen in this view beneath a large sign advertising Ward's Champion ales and stouts, brewed just across the Essex boundary at Foxearth. Later the old entrance was stopped up and the plaster was stripped away from the walls to reveal the timbering, giving the building a very different appearance.

BURY ST EDMUNDS

Bury St Edmunds largely owes its existence to the Benedictine monastery whose remains are still to be seen between the town and the River Lark. The precinct wall of the abbey is carried across the river on a twelfth-century bridge that has been the subject of generations of photographers. The body of King Edmund, who was probably killed by the Danes a few miles to the south at Bradfield St Clare rather than at the other sites mentioned by tradition, was brought to the abbey after his martyrdom in 869. His shrine attracted pilgrims both poor and rich in great numbers during the Middle Ages.

The Norman Gate was built under Abbot Anselm in the first half of the twelfth century to provide an entrance gate to the abbey church, an enormous building 50 ft longer than Norwich Cathedral. The relatively ornate decoration of the side facing the town made the gate, seen here at the beginning of the twentieth century after it had lost its battlements, a splendid entry for those on pilgrimage to the shrine of St Edmund who included royalty as well as the common people. After the destruction of the abbey the tower served as a campanile or bell tower for St James's Church, which in 1914 became the Cathedral of the new Diocese of St Edmundsbury and Ipswich.

A portrait of Sarah Fennell taken by Clarke & Wallace, of 28 Angel Hill, Bury St Edmunds, in May 1866 when she was aged ninety-one. Sarah, a member of the Society of Friends, left money to another member who used it to build four flats on land sold to her by the Bury Monthly Meeting. The intention was that the flats should be made available to 'respectable women in reduced circumstances, but with some income of their own, able and willing to read the Bible to the poor of Bury and to engage in other home-mission work as required'. The building in St Andrew's Street was probably the first purpose-built block of flats in the town.

Bury St Edmunds station is a somewhat imposing building that was still incomplete when first brought into use towards the end of 1847. It is seen here *c.* 1900, by which time the trainshed roof between the

two towers had been removed. Prominent in this view are the horse buses which met trains and took passengers to hotels in the town. (Suffolk Record Office)

King Edward VII and Queen Alexandra visited Bury St Edmunds on 17 December 1904, their visit being recorded by the local photographers whose pictures were hastily published as postcards. Above, the King is seen leaving St James's Church, and below his carriage, escorted by members of the Duke of York's (Loyal Suffolk Hussars) Suffolk Imperial Yeomanry, is turning from Angel Hill into Abbeygate Street. (John Wilton)

Little more than a month before the royal visit General Lord Methuen had unveiled a memorial to Suffolk men who had fallen in the South African War. By a strange coincidence the ceremony took place on 11 November, which was later to become Remembrance Day. The troops in light grey uniforms on the left are the Volunteers, members of the 2nd Volunteer Battalion, Suffolk Regiment; eight companies were based in Bury, with their headquarters at the Old Militia Barracks in Cemetery Road. Close by the memorial are a half-dozen newspaper reporters taking down Lord Methuen's speech. (John Wilton)

The corporation water cart on the left of this picture of Bury Market Place is sprinkling water to lay the dust. This is probably the Wednesday market, pictured *c.* 1908; the Saturday provision market filled the entire square. On the left, beyond the water cart, is Moyse's Hall, a stone-built house dating from the later twelfth century and traditionally said to have been originally the home of a Jew; there is no historical evidence to support this tradition. For many years it served as the Bridewell and the borough police station, but in 1899 it was opened as a museum. (John Wilton)

The Town Hall in Cornhill, seen in a frame from a ciné film made in Bury St Edmunds in 1913. Built on the site of the old Market Cross, destroyed with much of the town in a disastrous fire in 1608, it was used as a playhouse in which the Duke of Grafton's Comedians performed 'Bury Fair' in 1734. It was rebuilt in 1774 to the designs of Robert Adam. (East Anglian Film Archive)

Smith & Sons' shop at 37 and 38 Cornhill is prominent in the above view of Bury market some time before the First World War. A fine new street lamp has been erected, but in the photograph below taken in the 1920s the lamp post appears to be lightless. (John Wilton)

Abbeygate Street, Bury St Edmunds, in the 1920s, looking towards the Abbey Gate. Motor traffic has made its appearance, but there is still space enough for the errand boy to lean on his bicycle outside the outfitter's shop of Sidney Lodge (formerly Thomas Crick's) to watch the antics of the photographer. 'One looks over and across to The Mount (just under a mile away), yet with the feeling that but one stride and the romantic would have one foot in the heart of the town and the other among the trees in the country which surrounds it,' says Harry Marsh, a former mayor of Bury. 'A Ministry order has preserved this view for all time to the great disappointment of the "planners",' he adds.

The tradesmen of Bury as well as the townspeople generally turned out in force for the Lifeboat Saturday procession around the town in July 1906. The procession ended in the Lower Abbey Gardens, where these photographs were taken by one of the local photographers, who rapidly issued a set of postcards portraying the various floats. A pulling and sailing lifeboat on its launching carriage, which can just be seen in the lower picture on the opposite page, took part in the event. A pulling and sailing lifeboat is one that is dependent on oars and sail for propulsion, as opposed to a modern motor lifeboat. (John Wilton)

This pole waggon, a vehicle normally used for the transport of timber, has been used to accommodate one of the trade displays. Those staffing the float, who all seem to be dressed in their Sunday best under their carpenters' aprons, wear the folded paper hats traditionally worn by carpenters. To the left of the upper picture can be glimpsed the float of Robert Williams, saddler of Brentgovel Street, Bury, seen in its entirety below. (John Wilton)

One of the gems of Bury St Edmunds is the Theatre Royal, built in 1819 to the designs of the younger William Wilkins, son of the William Wilkins who had in 1799 obtained the lease of the theatres at Norwich, Colchester, Bury and Yarmouth. Its construction was financed by £100 subscriptions which entitled the subscriber to a silver ticket qualifying him to attend any performance he liked for the rest of his life as well as 5 per cent interest on his shares. After languishing for years as a barrel store for the local brewers the theatre was restored to its original use. Apart from being the only provincial Regency theatre surviving in its original structural form, it is remembered as the theatre that hosted the première of Brandon Thomas's play *Charley's Aunt*; the advertising card opposite reflects its long-running popularity. (John Wilton)

After the First World War a number of the original tanks were presented to various towns as war relics or memorials. This one in the Abbey Gardens at Bury is seen in a postcard sent home in 1923 to a farmer's wife at Newbourne, near Woodbridge, by her young brother who had just enlisted in the Suffolk Regiment at Bury's Gibraltar Barracks. 'Sorry I have not written before,' he writes, 'but we got our equipment and I have been busy cleaning it up.' In his years of service, which took him to the Far East and to China, he no doubt spent many hours polishing and blancoing his equipment. The first tanks were sent to a training camp at Elveden, about ten miles north of Bury, where crews and machines were put through their paces before being sent to France. (Mrs Marion Leeson)

THE LARK & LITTLE OUSE

The River Lark was made navigable to Bury St Edmunds so that coal and other goods could be brought upriver from the port of King's Lynn. On the river lies Mildenhall, whose Market Cross is seen here in a photograph taken in about 1910. At left can be seen the shop of Harry F. Ungless, fancy draper, which after his death in 1906 was run by Mrs Ungless, who was a milliner. Lying near the edge of the Fens, Mildenhall is the largest parish in Suffolk and contains a number of outlying hamlets. A probable reason for the parish being so extensive is that much of the land was marginal and a large area was needed to support the population.

The red-brick Tudor gatehouse of West Stow Hall, near where the Icknield Way crosses the River Lark, with its octagonal corner turrets bearing the arms of Henry VIII's sister Mary Tudor, Queen of France and Duchess of Suffolk, who is buried in St Mary's Church at Bury St Edmunds. At the time this photograph was taken in the 1890s the hall was the home of Henry Frost, Earl Cadogan's agent. (Mrs M. Leeson)

Looking across the Market Place at Mildenhall in the 1920s, with the cycle shop of D. Cattermole, formerly Mrs Mabel Kemp's and earlier William Kemp's, on the right. The premises of a saddler and harnessmaker, Isaac Minns, is just beyond. Dominating the background is the fifteenth-century tower of St Mary's Church.

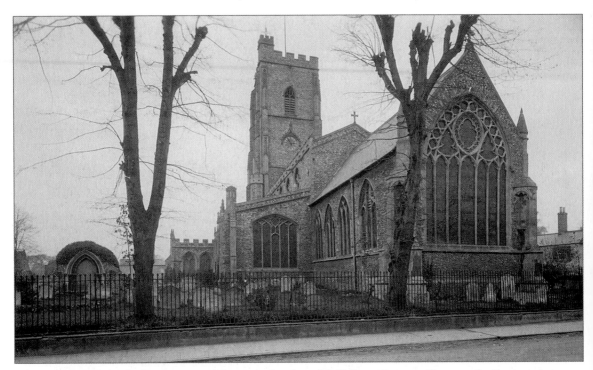

Mildenhall parish church is one of the great churches of Suffolk, with a magnificent roof whose angels bear the marks of shot supposedly fired at them by Puritan soldiers. The tracery of the east window, well seen in this view, is somewhat remarkable, and the mighty tower, completed by 1464, is a landmark for miles around; until 1831 it was capped by a lantern and spirelet, which would have given it an even more impressive appearance.

Mildenhall High Street *c.* 1910, with the Tiger's Head and the shop of Henry Matthew Burt, bookseller, stationer and printer, on the right. It is quite possible that this and other views in the same series were taken by a visiting photographer and reproduced as postcards for sale in Burt's shop. There were several firms which were in the business of producing postcards for such local shops.

A view of High Street and the church tower from the Market Place taken in the 1930s. The imposing house seen in the photograph on page 133 has been turned into a pair of shops, the right-hand one of which is run by Henry Montague Stiles, outfitter; the other, named Lucille, was run by the Misses N. and P. Sewell. The building on the left, seen also in the previous illustration, has had the plaster stripped off to reveal the timbering and has become Barclays Bank.

The deep gutters in Mill Street, Mildenhall, are bridged by cast-iron channels outside each door in this 1920s view, looking towards High Street. The car parked by the edge of the road bears an early West Suffolk registration, CF-3131 (note the hyphen).

The Lark enters the Great Ouse between Prickwillow and Littleport, and the Little Ouse has its confluence with the major river a few miles downstream at Brandon Creek. Barges could travel up the Little Ouse to Brandon and Thetford through a number of staunches like the one at Brandon, above. In the picture below of Brandon bridge two sunken lighters provide a foreground feature for the photographer. (John Wilton)

These Edwardian youngsters fishing from the old bridge at Brandon, or watching others fishing, attracted Jarrolds' photographer as he travelled round seeking subjects for his firm's postcards. Old warehouses and maltings beside the river provide evidence of a waterborne trade that had already come to an end.

IN THE WEST

Haverhill had a population of little more than 3,000 in the nineteenth century, yet it was a thriving town whose main employers, Gurteen & Sons, had a workforce of more than 2,500 in 1879. This view of the junction of Wratting Road and Withersfield Road in the 1890s shows the premises of James Henderson, ropemaker, and on the right the Rose and Crown Hotel. In the foreground is a two-horse coal cart belonging to the Haverhill Industrial Co-operative Society. (Haverhill & District Local History Group)

Haverhill High Street in 1868, with the Bell Hotel in the middle of the picture and Gurteen's office next-door. The buildings on the left were in the churchyard. The shop on the extreme right became the Coffee Tavern in 1880, as can be seen in the picture on the opposite page. (Haverhill & District Local History Group)

Looking the other way along Haverhill High Street in the 1880s, with The Anchor Coffee Tavern and Dining Rooms, otherwise known as the Coffee Tavern for short, on the left in rather uncomfortable proximity to the yard occupied by Greene & Son, the Bury St Edmunds brewers. The Temperance movement inaugurated coffee taverns and similar establishments in many towns in an endeavour to attract working men away from the public houses. On the right are Chauntry House, then the residence of the senior Daniel Gurteen, and Market Hill Chapel, which is now a shop. The photographer is not recorded, but the picture was issued by Chevens & Son, printers of 25 High Street, as were others of the town at this period. (Haverhill & District Local History Group)

Haverhill High Street towards the end of the nineteenth century, with the 1889 Corn Exchange on the left (labelled 'Furniture Warehouse'). The horse van belongs to William Byford, who besides being a corn

and coal merchant operated as a carrier between the town and the local railway stations. (Haverhill & District Local History Group)

This photograph of Haverhill Brass Band was taken in 1889 by local photographer Charles Mizon, who was himself a band member. At the time of this photograph they were wearing military-style helmets with brass spikes, but an earlier photograph shows the bandsmen, including Mizon, wearing soft-topped peaked caps. (Haverhill & District Local History Group)

There were three windmills in Haverhill, the best remembered being the big mid-nineteenth-century tower mill that stood to the north of the town until its demolition in 1942. The miller, Richard Ruffle, designed his own annular sail which was some 50 ft in diameter with 120 5-ft vanes, basing it on the invention of an Essex miller, Henry Chopping. This mill worked until 1933, when it suffered damage which put it out of action.

Only St Mary's Church survives of the buildings shown on this photograph of Peas Hill, Haverhill, issued in the 1880s by Chevens & Son. The bystanders have all been warned to remain still while the exposure is taken; it is remarkable that not one face is blurred. (Haverhill & District Local History Group)

The Haverhill celebrations of Queen Victoria's Diamond Jubilee in 1897 photographed by George Moss, who succeeded Charles Mizon as the local photographer during the mid-1890s. A variety of fancy dress is worn by the cyclists in the foreground. The significance of Daniel Maynard Gurteen being dressed as a pig in a smock is forgotten, but the smock would have been one of those made by his family firm. (Haverhill & District Local History Group)

Haverhill's younger generation gathers as the photographer sets up his camera on its tripod in the middle of High Street one day in the 1890s. Few of them heeded his warning to keep still, and the picture is somewhat marred by the many blurs that have resulted. The east end of St Mary's Church can be seen in the distance beyond Chauntry House; on the right is the Red Lion, supplied by P.L. Hudson's brewery at Pampisford in Cambridgeshire. The solitary street light was one of those lit by gas from the gasworks set up in 1854 and acquired by the local authority in 1886. (Haverhill & District Local History Group)

Spring cleaning in Edwardian Haverhill: carpets from The Mount, to which Daniel Maynard Gurteen had moved from Chauntry House, are being cleaned on the tennis lawn by, it is thought, William Webb, Freddie Ford, Bill Reede and Freddie Ford's father. In the background can be seen the Old Independent Congregational Church, which was attended by the Gurteen family. (Haverhill & District Local History Group)

Haverhill Brass Band sets off at 2 p.m. from outside the Old Rectory, later known as Anne of Cleves House, at the head of the procession organized to celebrate the Coronation of King George V in 1911. The celebrations had started in the morning with the ringing of church bells and firing of guns, the ceremonial signing of a loyal address by the urban district council and a thanksgiving service in St Mary's Church. This and the following photographs were almost certainly taken by a member of the Gurteen family and were given to the Haverhill & District Local History Group by Miss Grace Gurteen. (Haverhill & District Local History Group)

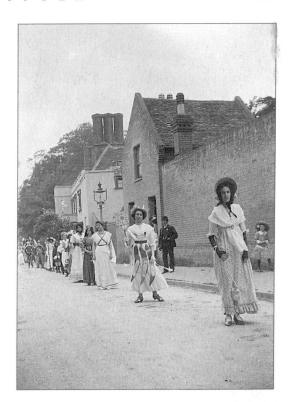

One section of the coronation procession was for ladies in period costume; entrants are seen on the right setting off along Hamlet Road. (Haverhill & District Local History Group)

This entry, on a wagon owned by Gurteen & Son, was a group of 'Druids'. The costumes had been used two years earlier in a pageant of religious history presented by the Haverhill and District Sunday School Union. (Haverhill & District Local History Group)

Haverhill Fire Brigade, whose fire station was in Duddery Road, are seen here outside the Old Rectory with their manual fire engine as they take part in the coronation procession; they won first prize in their section. (Haverhill & District Local History Group)

Celia Smart, Grace Gurteen and Joyce Boardman in their Cinderella costumes in the Gurteen family's car, which had been decorated for the coronation procession. Chauffeur William Webb was apprehensive as the radiator nearly boiled over, either because of the swan decoration blocking the air flow or because he had to drive slowly along the processional route. (Haverhill & District Local History Group)

Newmarket has been known as the capital of horseracing since King Charles II came to the town to enjoy racing on the heath. In the postcard picture of *c.* 1912 above the only traffic at the south end of High Street is a string of horses. At left an employee of Newmarket Urban District Council stands by his handcart. In the picture below of the High Street by the White Hart one gets a hint of the traffic problems that were to come with the advent of the motor-car; the main road from Norwich to London ran through the town.

The Rowley Mile racecourse on Newmarket Heath, *c.* 1912. (John Wilton)

The clock tower at the north end of Newmarket High Street was erected to commemorate Queen Victoria's golden jubilee in 1887. When this photograph was taken, before the outbreak of the First World War, the clock tower seemed to fit into the scene, but today it has, as Norman Scarfe puts it, 'merely been turned into a traffic roundabout'.

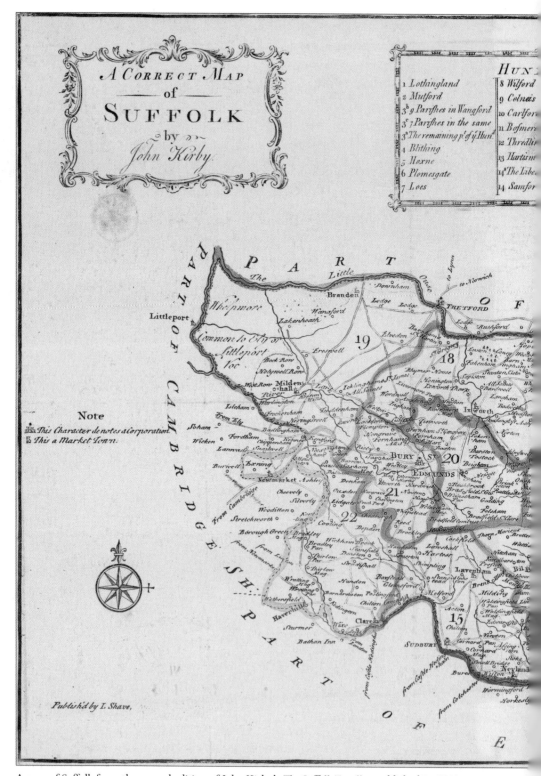

A map of Suffolk from the second edition of John Kirby's *The Suffolk Traveller*, published in 1764.

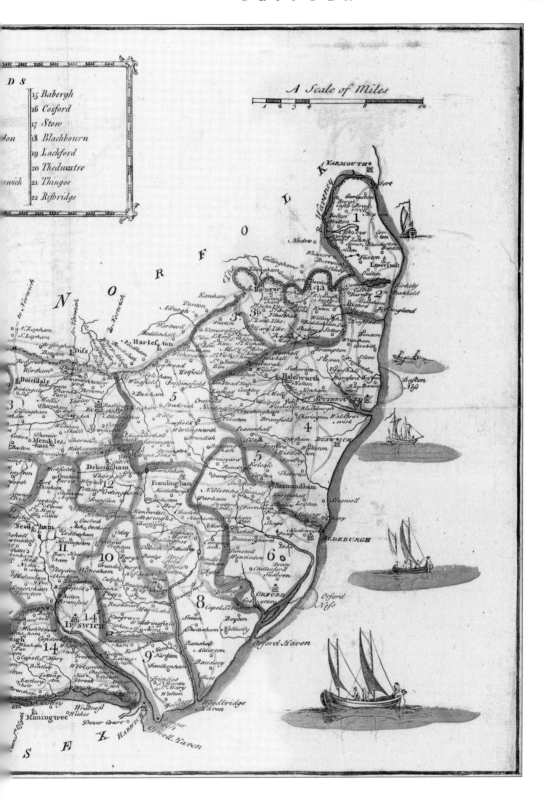